SALAMATI

HAMED'S PERSIAN KITCHEN

HAMED ALLAHYARI WITH DANI VALENT

SALAMATI
HAMED'S PERSIAN KITCHEN

*Recipes and stories from Iran to
the other side of the world*

Interlink Books

An imprint of Interlink Publishing Group, Inc.
Northampton, Massachusetts

*"This book is a feast for the heart, soul, and spirit.
A book to cherish with recipes made with love and humanity."*

Kon Karapanagiotidis, CEO and founder of the Asylum Seeker Resource Center

Foreword

The reason I love writing about food, the reason it's so enriching and everlastingly interesting, is that it connects me with wonderful people through a topic that is at the core of who they are. It's direct and meaningful. So it was when I first met Hamed and felt the poignant immersion in culture that he expresses in his cooking. To be able to go deeper, to write with him, to help him bring his story to life, has been an honor and a privilege. I've learned so much. Not just about saffron and rice and eggplants and herbs, but also about fortitude and resilience and spirit. Hamed fled Iran suddenly, with nothing. The recipes in his heart and hands became key belongings, a refugee's anchor to home and hopeful gift to his new country.

To work on this book during a pandemic was a particular challenge: we did a lot on the phone, I sent Hamed photos of dishes I'd cooked, and when we could finally be together in person for the photoshoot, it was a joyous rush of sights, smells, and textures, shared at last. To write this book has been Hamed's dream for a long time. I feel so lucky to be part of it.

DANI VALENT

Dedicated with love
to my country and the
people of Iran

Contents

Introduction

Hamed Allahyari cooks to connect. The food of his native Iran is a resonant and delicious gift and a way of staying bonded to a country he hasn't returned to for a decade. With every swipe of warm lavash through herbed dadami dip, every bite of braised lamb with dried lime and saffron rice, and every sip of house-made sour cherry tea, Hamed shines a light on his Persian past as he continues to build an optimistic future.

In Iran, Hamed was a chef and restaurateur when a crisis of faith imperiled his life. Atheism is illegal in the Islamic Republic and disobeying the tenets of Islam is a crime. One day Hamed was seen smoking a cigarette during Ramadan—he was arrested and received 80 lashes. Once idealistic and hopeful, by 2012 Hamed came to realize that leaving his country—immediately—was his only option.

There was no time to tell his family but he met his girlfriend Elahe to say goodbye. She greeted him with a positive pregnancy test and in the moment they decided to leave together. They traveled to Indonesia where they were stuck for two uncertain months, then sailed by rickety fishing boat towards Australia where they were detained on Christmas Island. After five months of detention, Hamed and Elahe were released into the Melbourne community and a few months after that their daughter Nikan Rose was born.

It was natural for Hamed to gravitate towards food after his perilous escape and journey to Australia. His first dream was to find work: without English or local experience, that was hard enough. His next ambition was to open a business: his heartfelt cafe and restaurant

SalamaTea launched in 2019. This intimate, colorful restaurant in the suburbs of Melbourne is a hard-won sanctuary and a place for sharing his pride in Persian cooking. People come for tea, talk, and baghlava, family groups share fesenjun with chicken and walnuts, tradespeople stop by for sandwiches and Anzac cookies made with Hamed's special Persian touch. As soon as he could, Hamed employed fellow refugees and asylum seekers at SalamaTea, giving them the work experience that he found so hard to come by himself.

The culmination of all his toil and passion is this book, the testament that brings it all together, celebrating the cuisine that nurtured him in childhood, gave him his first career in Iran, and enabled him to build a new life in Australia.

Hamed's food is anchored in tradition but accessible to all. The recipes are simple, appealing, and full of flavor, redolent of stories as well as spices. Many of the dishes in this book are on the menu at SalamaTea; others have been road-tested at hundreds of cooking classes and catering events. Hamed melds Persian culinary culture and an understanding of western palates to create recipes that are truly his—and now ours—to share.

Beyond the recipes, this book is a gateway to Persia. "It's sharing my culture," says Hamed. "It's my dream that everyone tries Persian food. And with my food, they come into my family. They are sitting with me, with my grandparents, parents, brothers and sister, and cousins, talking, sharing, and enjoying the feeling of being together." —DANI VALENT

Dani Valent and
Hamed Allahyari

My Life in Food

When I think back to my earliest days, my memories are always around food: preparing it and eating it, always wanting to be in the middle of the communal nature of eating in Iran, anchored in tradition and romanced by flavor. It was just in me somehow.

I'm the youngest in my family and I was always up first—not that I'm a morning person at all! The job of the first person awake is "dam kardan e chai," which means getting the tea ready. Every Iranian household has the kettle on the whole day. In the old days, it was a samovar over a charcoal fire. These days, it's a tin kettle that is always simmering on the smallest gas flame; on top of that is a teapot brewing black tea all day. The teapot never boils but is gently heated by the steam of the kettle. It's not a Persian home without this double-decker set-up!

I would get up and put the water on and then I would bother my mom sleeping in her bed and ask her for money to go and buy bread. Every neighborhood has a bakery and it's very typical for an Iranian household to buy fresh bread each morning. Mom would sleepily tell me to take money from her bag and I would run off for just-baked flatbread.

When I got back, I'd arrange our breakfast: bread, cheese, walnuts, butter, tahini, grape molasses, all spread out on our sofreh, the special cloth we lay on the floor to eat around. I wasn't allowed to use the kettle when I was little, but as soon as everyone got up Mom would make the first tea, chai shireen, a sweet tea to start the day. She would be excited to see the food laid out and I loved that she loved that I'd do that.

Every day, I'd ask my mother, "What are you going to cook?" "What is for lunch?" "What is for dinner?" And if I didn't have homework, I'd be next to her in the kitchen, stirring, frying onions, taking on small responsibilities. If my father was making kebabs on the weekends, I'd be there. "You go sit, Baba, I will make it."

My father was an army general and the apartment we lived in was in a complex of eight buildings with 160 army families all living together. We would play soccer and volleyball and go to our mosque. Food was a big part of religious life. During festivals, such as Muharram and Ramadan, the mosque would feed thousands of people for free. We had a head chef and all the boys in the community would help. There'd be 10 of us standing in a line peeling 100 kilograms (220 pounds) of onions, crying together. I loved to be involved. I remember looking at our rice pots proudly: we had 10 big pots, each holding 100 kilograms (220 pounds) of rice. The scale was immense. I'm not religious anymore but I do miss the communal nature of those Islamic festivals, and if I ever have the chance to cook for a lot of people, I jump at it. >

✽ *Dishes cooked at the mosque:*
GHEYMEH BADEMJAN *page 130*
ZERESHK POLOW BA MORGH *page 125*
ADAS POLOW *page 168*
SHOLEZARD *page 201*

As much as I loved to be involved in food, it would be a stretch to say that I really knew how to cook. That changed when I moved away from home. It was actually quite unusual to move to a shared house—most people in Iran stay living at home until they get married. But I had a lot of conflict with my father. He would wake me up every day at 6 am to pray and I didn't want to. He was always pushing me but I just wasn't into religion. In Iran, that's a really big deal. It's illegal to not be an observant Muslim—it's why I eventually had to flee the country and start my new life in Australia. I didn't want to fight with my father so, when I was 19, after my army service, I decided it was best to live separately and I moved into a house with some friends.

Typical boys, we lived on junk food for the first few months. After a while I offered to cook for everyone in exchange for a rent reduction and they all agreed. We were all so sick of spending money on fast food. I started making makaroni (Persian-style spaghetti) and omelets, simple dishes I remembered from home. One day we invited some friends over to play cards and I decided to make ash reshteh, our famous Persian noodle soup.

❋ *Dishes cooked at share house:*
OMELETS *pages 27–34*
PERSIAN MAKARONI WITH TAHDIG *page 154*
ASH RESHTEH *page 102*

I called my mother at every step. First she told me all the ingredients: lentils, kidney beans, onions, spices, noodles, and lots and lots of herbs. Luckily, below our place there was a herb shop, which is a common type of store in Iran. When you want to make a dish like ash reshteh or ghormeh sabzi (slow-cooked lamb with herbs), you can buy the enormous quantities of herbs needed, chopped and ready to go. It makes a huge difference when someone else washes, picks, and chops your herbs. At the same shop, you can also buy homemade verjuice and fresh lemon juice. You simply take a bottle and the shop owner fills it up. It's very handy.

I then called my mom to talk me through the process—I just put the turmeric in, what now? And she would explain it very slowly, all the details, lots of tips, very calm. She is a great teacher. I served the ash to my friends and they all said it was amazing. I felt really proud in that moment. After that my friends started telling me about the dishes their mothers made and I would call my mom and ask her how to cook them. She knew all the dishes and she passed on the recipes. In that house, I learned to cook very well.

A few months later, I had the great opportunity to work at Hyperstar, a huge supermarket with a restaurant, deli, pastry shop, and bakery. It was a really different concept for Iran; even the fact that they could use English words in their name was new. It was here that I saw my first croissant, my first avocado, my first hummus. I started in the bakery making croissants, layering the butter, using the laminating machine. Then I moved next door to the traditional bakery where we made Iranian bread, and next I worked in the kitchen where we sold classic Persian fare, such as tahchin and jujeh kababs, thousands a day, as well as dishes like fesenjun and ghormeh sabzi.

✽ *Dishes cooked at Hyperstar:*
NOON LAVASH *page 57*
TAHCHIN *page 120*
JUJEH KABAB *page 153*
FESENJUN *page 116*
BAGHLAVA *page 192*

I moved from station to station, always learning. I was constantly hungry for the next skill, the next recipe. During my time at Hyperstar I sneakily learned to make baghlava, watching over the shoulder of a chef who had been making it for 30 years. He was mad at me because after two weeks, I could do it just like him. But I'd realized I loved cooking, I wanted to be good at it, so I soaked up the opportunity to learn from professionals and on a large scale.

After a couple of years at Hyperstar, I wanted to do my own thing, so with two friends I took over a ghahveh khaneh (coffee house) in Jajrud, outside of Tehran, on a busy road to the north. We say "coffee house" but actually the main focus in a ghahveh khaneh is tea and shisha, the water tobacco pipes that are so popular in Iran. All shisha places serve tomato omelets but my menu was a bit bigger than usual. People would make the 50 minute drive from Tehran especially to eat my ghormeh sabzi.

✽ *Dishes cooked at coffee house:*
GHAHVE KHUNEE OMELET *page 34*
GHORMEH SABZI *page 133*

It was a really fun, exciting, and satisfying time for me as a cook, but there were other things going on in my life, too. You already know that as a teenager I didn't want to get up early to go and pray, mostly because I was lazy. But as a young man, I started to identify more strongly as an atheist as I started meeting and talking to more people, opening my mind.

Here, it's no big deal to not believe in God. But in Iran, it's enormous. You can be imprisoned or even killed for it. In Iran, there are two types of police: the regular police and the religious police (The Islamic Revolutionary Guards, Sepah Pasdaran, backed up by the Basij militia). The religious police will arrest you, and flog you, if they see you drinking water or smoking during the Ramadan fasts. They will arrest women for not wearing the hijab properly. I was often in trouble with them. Looking back, I was so idealistic. It didn't cross my mind that my activities would lead to me fleeing my homeland.

The situation got very dramatic very quickly and I was scared. We were a small underground group—it was just meetings, some small actions; nothing violent or anything. We believed the government would change and there would be more freedoms, freedom to be ourselves, but it wasn't to be. Four of the young men in our group disappeared—even to this day their families don't know what happened to them. We were out of our depth and extremely frightened. A friend told me to go to Australia, that it was a good country with good people. "Australia" was just a word I'd heard in school but it seemed like the only option. My friend advised me to go to Jakarta, as if for a vacation, and then go by boat to Australia. >

I went to say goodbye to my girlfriend, Elahe. I told her I was in danger and that I needed to leave. She had just at that moment taken a pregnancy test—it was positive. My mind was swirling: I was going to be a father, I was leaving my country. In the moment, we decided to go together and without having time to say goodbye to my family, we flew to Indonesia.

We spent two uncertain months in a motel in Jakarta, waiting to be smuggled to Australia. It was a hard time, full of disappointment and bribes and danger, but we had no choice but to trust and hope. Eventually, we were crowded onto a truck and bounced our way to the sea where we were crammed onto a small boat for the two-day journey to Christmas Island. It was hugely risky and a strange feeling to have no control over my life in that moment. But even on that boat, wondering if I would die, I was glad to take my chance. I felt like it would have been better to die in the ocean in the mouth of a shark than be hanged in terror by my own government.

We were on Christmas Island for five months, waiting to be let into Australia after having sought asylum. It wasn't too bad for me, partly because we had English classes. I had never learned English beyond, "Hello! How are you? What time is it?" I was planning to live in Iran my whole life; it never occurred to me I would need another language. We were released with a bridging visa and went to Melbourne. The visa conditions meant I couldn't work, I couldn't study. It was very tough, actually. My daughter, Nikan Rose, arrived four months after we came to Melbourne, but I couldn't work to support her and Elahe. There was a tiny amount of government support but every day was a

Through my dishes, my cooking classes, and my restaurant, I am proud to introduce my culture to people.

struggle to make ends meet. After two years I got a new bridging visa with employment rights, so I immediately started studying English and looking for work. I was a chef in Iran but no one was looking for a Persian chef in Melbourne and I didn't have any references, no one to vouch for me. I didn't get a single job offer from 50 or 60 ads, until finally I was offered a dishwashing job for AUS $8 (about US $6) an hour. No way, I thought!

I took a different path. I saw that the problem was that I didn't have a resume that meant anything in Australia, so I decided to get some experience by volunteering. I went to the Asylum Seeker Resource Center in Footscray, a place that helps refugees and people seeking asylum with all sorts of things, from legal advice to food. Every day they feed 250 people a free lunch. I started cooking there two days a week, making Persian food for people from all over the world: Sri Lanka, Afghanistan, Myanmar, Sierra Leone, all kinds of places, and most of them had never tried Persian food before. But when they tried it, they liked it. They talked to me about it, asked me about it, and it made me so happy.

After a while, people suggested I try cooking classes. I was unsure—I had never been a teacher—but a long time had passed since I was that 19-year-old boy on the phone to my mother, stumbling my way through making ash reshteh. I was put in touch with Free to Feed, a social enterprise that works with refugees. It was an amazing opportunity for me. I started with one class a week and it grew and grew, until some weeks I was teaching three classes. Over the years, more than 2500 people ended up coming to learn about Persian food. One by one, I was sharing my culture and it was a beautiful feeling. I was working, I was teaching, and I was also learning. I started asking my students for feedback—was it delicious for them?—and building an understanding of what they liked to eat. People kept asking if I could cater for their events, or if I had a restaurant they could visit. In time, I started both. No one would give me a job in Australia so I had to give myself a job! But I didn't forget my early hardships looking for work. I created my businesses as social enterprises, employing other asylum seekers and refugees, helping them create a resume and references that would put them on the path to a new life. My restaurant is in Sunshine, a very multicultural western suburb of Melbourne. I opened it in 2019 and called it SalamaTea, a play on the Persian "salamati," which means "cheers" and also "health." I hope that everyone who walks through the doors feels my warm welcome.

Being a refugee is not easy, and I still don't have a permanent visa, but after many years I truly feel like I have found my place. I have a life here, a rich life where I can be myself. Through my dishes, my cooking classes, and my restaurant, I am proud to introduce my culture to people. I love to share the stories and the recipes that are part of who I am—and also part of the heritage of my two Australian-born children, Nikan Rose and my son Kian, who was born in 2016. It's such a good feeling when people like the dishes I've made. It sustains me and keeps me warm and inspired.

To me, cooking is art and chefs are artists. Cooking is my gift and I think it's right that I use that gift to feed the people around me. A barber cuts your hair and makes you beautiful. A gardener grows flowers and makes the garden beautiful. I cook for humanity and make the world a more beautiful place in that way. Food is my gift and I want to give it to you, whether it's at my table or through the pages of this book.

Salamati!

My Country, My Persia

I like to say I'm from Persia rather than Iran. For me, Persia is culture and romance, spice trails and silk roads, a rich heritage of farming, cooking, and gathering around food. Iran, on the other hand, has connotations of the Islamic Republic founded in 1979. It's a word bound up in the politics of the regime that caused me to leave my home, in a hurry and in danger, in 2012. I am Iranian but my heart is Persian. In truth, the two words are used almost interchangeably. "Iran" has the same roots as the word "aryan" and can be traced back to at least the third century AD. Iran means "land of the Aryans," and it has encapsulated the various Persian empires that have swelled and shrunk over the centuries, a dynamic mingling of people, language, religion and, of course, food.

Today's Iran sits at the junction of the Indian subcontinent, Central Asia, Eastern Europe, and the Middle East. To the south-east is Pakistan and beyond it India; to the east and north we encounter the "stans" of central Asia: Afghanistan and Turkmenistan, along with the Caspian Sea; to the north-west, there's Azerbaijan, Armenia, and Turkey; and finally to the west and south you'll find the Middle Eastern countries of Iraq and the Gulf States across the Persian Gulf. It's a rich, complex, storied region and you can easily imagine the great interplay of produce, flavors, and cooking styles.

In many people's minds, Persian food is bound up in the whole idea of Middle Eastern food, but the cuisine is quite distinct. You might be surprised to learn that I'd never eaten hummus until I was 20! Of course, there are many points of intersection with the food of the Arabs, who conquered Iran in the seventh century AD, but there are also Ottoman influences, Indian flavors, and Zoroastrian lore and ingredients, which found their way along the long trade routes from China and beyond.

When you grow up in Iran, you find it all very natural, this never-ending banquet at the intersection of the Silk Road, threaded with Islamic celebrations, Zoroastrian festivals, harvest traditions, and family habits. It's a cuisine that is often humble in essence but with a love of lavish flourishes, and always served with pride, no matter how simple it might be. In my experience, whatever the setting and whatever the heritage, Persian food comes from the heart—and now from my heart to your home.

خنک آن دم که نشینیم در ایوان من و تو

به دو نقش و به دو صورت به یکی جان من و تو

Khonak an dam ke neshinim dar eyvan, man o to

Be do naghsho be do soorat, be yeki jan, man o to

The pleasant moment of sitting in front of the door, me and you

With two figures and two faces, with one life, me and you

مولانا رومی

Molana Rumi

Persian Food Culture

How we eat

The Iranian table is all about accumulation, with dishes added as we eat rather than a series of staged courses. We don't really serve dessert to finish a meal, though we certainly love to eat sweets at any time of day. As it happens, sweet and savory elements are very often combined in one dish: there's the pomegranate molasses in a stew, the saffron that's ground with sugar and added to polows (pilafs), the sweet–sour bite of barberries.

Traditionally we eat around a sofreh, a special cloth (or sometimes a sheet of colorful plastic) that's laid over a Persian carpet on the floor. It's not a home without a sofreh. It is only used for food and, even though it's on the ground, everyone takes care not to stand on it.

All the food and drink is laid on the cloth and we sit around to eat. Some people also spread a sofreh on a table and eat around that but, honestly, we love the floor and we are comfortable sitting with our legs crossed.

It's worth mentioning that shoes are taken off when entering a home. Often, guests will be offered slippers, but otherwise socks or bare feet are fine.

How we cook

Naturally, there are weights and measures in this cookbook but most people in Iran tend to cook without strict instructions. I never saw my mother with a kitchen scale. We tend to eat seasonally, choosing staples from the pantry—huge sacks of rice and dried legumes—that are then boosted with fresh herbs and vegetables.

Food is often seen as medicinal and there is a big reliance on family lore and traditions around healing foods. If I felt sick, my mother would often start making a dish thought to boost immunity or fight an infection. The main paradigm is around foods that are considered "hot" or "cold." This has nothing to do with temperature but is more about balancing the body's metabolism. For example, rice is considered "cold" (even if it's served hot) and saffron is considered "hot," so they are often served together to balance each other.

It's not something I think about actively as I cook or design menus, but I do think it accounts for the innate harmony of many dishes in this book. There's something about the ingredients in Persian dishes that feels like they want to be together.

A word on presentation

Much of the drama and contrast of Iranian dishes comes from the garnishes, flourishes, and accompaniments: a sprinkle of sumac, a hidden burst of barberries, the dark fried onions, or sprinkling of pomegranate molasses or arils scattered over a dish. Persian cooks let time slow down as they carefully finish a dish, making the most of color and contrast to turn every meal into a special occasion.

A note on alcohol

Alcohol is banned in Iran but that doesn't mean people don't drink it. There are bootleg dealers that deliver alcohol and some people make arak at home from fermented raisins. Because it's forbidden, I found drinking exciting and fun. There is a thrilling edge to parties in Iran.

Essential Ingredients & Cooking Techniques

❋ *Aloo Bokhara*

This special plum, usually sold as a dried fruit, has a deep plummy flavor and is prized because it's both sour and sweet. Aloo bokhara can be hard to find, even in Iran, and dried apricots are a reasonable alternative.

❋ *Barberries*

You can't think of Persian cuisine without barberries, which we call zereshk. They're prized for their sour pop of flavor and because they look like shiny jewels scattered through a dish. We buy them dried and usually rehydrate them before adding to dishes. It's not always easy to find barberries outside of Iran. You can use dried cranberries or apricots instead, but they don't have the same piquant sourness of barberries.

❋ *Golpar*

Heracleum persicum, sometimes called Persian hogweed or angelica, is a key herb in Persian cooking. It has a particular fragrant bitterness and can be purchased dried and ground from Middle Eastern supermarkets and online. If you can't find it, just leave it out; there's really no substitute.

❋ *Herbs*

No one loves herbs quite like Iranians. A meal is unthinkable without them. We eat them raw, we eat them cooked, and we use them in enormous quantities. We really don't understand those tiny bunches or plastic containers of herbs in Western markets—it's not enough! In Iran, every shopping strip has a store dedicated to herbs and you can buy them by the armful.

The classic preparation of mixed greens—mostly herbs, but also radishes and scallions—is called Sabzi Khordan (page 214).

❋ *Kashk*

A fermented dairy product that's very important in Persian cuisine, especially in classic dishes, such as Ash Reshteh (page 102). Kashk can be made from yogurt or the whey left over from cheesemaking. It is sold in liquid form or dehydrated and sold as a powder, to be reconstituted into liquid at home. It's a real flavor bomb!

❋ *Persian dried limes*

We dry limes until they are black and so light they feel hollow. Their deep sour flavor is extracted during a long, slow braise—use a fork to puncture the limes before adding to a dish.

❋ *Pomegranates*

This magical orb is Iran's national fruit, a symbol of abundance and a point of pride for our farming communities. Pomegranates are grown in large quantities and there are many varieties with arils of different colors and sizes. We scatter these juicy jewels over polows (pilafs) and salads, and we use pomegranate molasses—a syrupy reduction of the juice—in many savory braises, bringing a sweet–sour tang to a dish.

My trick for removing the arils is to cut the fruit into quarters and hold each piece over a bowl with the arils facing down. Using a tablespoon, tap briskly and firmly on the skin so the seeds drop into the bowl.

On Yalda Night (winter solstice), it's traditional to eat a special pomegranate snack. We mix the seeds with salt and golpar (see left) and eat it with a spoon. Sometimes, we'll make this snack and eat it like popcorn if we're watching a movie, too.

✺ Rice

The way we make rice is very particular. We generally use long-grain basmati rice. We soak it, drain it, boil it until it's mostly cooked, then drain it again and mix it with other polow (pilaf) ingredients. We then finish cooking it slowly with oil to create a tahdig (see right).

✺ Saffron

We love saffron in Persia. These tiny strands—plucked from the crocus flower—are a luxury that bring color, fragrance, and special flavor to so many dishes, both savory and sweet. It's not cheap but a little goes a long way.

To make the most of saffron, it's important to prepare it properly to extract the maximum flavor and color. My usual method is to grind a tiny pinch of saffron threads in a mortar and pestle with a tablespoon of sugar. The sugar acts like tiny grindstones and the saffron threads easily turn to powder. I then add a splash of boiling water to melt the sugar and extract the color. This burnished red-gold liquid is then added to dishes. For a recipe, turn to page 214.

✺ Sumac

These beautifully fragrant red flakes are made from the sumac berry that is commonly grown in Iran. Sumac is loved for the fragrant lemony notes it brings to dishes and also because it looks so shiny and pretty scattered over a dish.

✺ Tahdig

One of the most spectacular and essential features of Persian cuisine is the tahdig, the golden, crunchy bottom of a rice polow (pilaf). In its simplest form, the tahdig forms from the rice itself. But it can also be made from flatbread or sliced potato, or a mix of the two, then layered under almost-cooked rice and gently fried over a very low heat until the base is golden and crunchy. In addition to flatbread and potato, you can also use vegetables, such as lettuce, eggplant, and zucchini.

Tahdig can be eaten as it comes out of the pan, with the rice scooped out to reveal the tahdig treasure beneath, but the pan can also be inverted, turning the tahdig into a spectacular crunchy lid. It's so much easier to have success with this if you use a nonstick sauté pan. You can only ever make a small amount of tahdig—a thin layer the size of your pan base—and it's never enough. In my family, it's the first thing we all eat. We try to save it but it's impossible—everyone attacks the crunchy golden shards!

✺ Tilit

When we soak bread in a thin soup, we call it tilit. It turns a light snack into a meal. I always add bread to the chilled yogurt soup Abdoogh Khiar (page 101) and Kaleh Joosh (page 109), a potato and split pea soup. Tilit can be plain, torn flatbread but fried bread gives an even better flavor.

Most days, people in Iran have a very simple breakfast. We start with black tea, then eat bread with butter and jam, or cream and honey, or walnuts and feta. We'll often have our ubiquitous herb platter, Sabzi Khordan (page 214), too. Our first cup of tea is sweet but the second cup is usually plain.

When we have a little more time, omelets are very popular, so that's what I've focused on in this chapter. I love the variety of Persian omelets: they can be sweet or savory and are always served with herbs on the side. I'm sharing my own technique for cooking them, separating the yolks and whites in the pan and cooking the whites first to create perfect just-cooked eggs.

In Iran we also have a collection of pan-cooked egg dishes called kuku. These are thicker—more like Spanish omelets—and you'll find them in the Appetizers, Sides & Street Food chapter (page 62).

There's one Iranian breakfast recipe that I've decided not to share here and I think you'll probably forgive me! It's kaleh pacheh (head and hoof), a special braise of sheep's head, tongue, cheek, eye, brain, and foot. It's made in dedicated shops and served early on Fridays (our weekend), either for eating in or taking home. The meat is rich and tender, a bit like lamb shank, and we season it with cinnamon and lemon juice. I love it— maybe I'll put it in my next book!

Brunch

Dadami Breakfast

My father, Ali-Abbas, was an army general but he's been retired now for nearly 20 years. Even when he was working he enjoyed cooking, which was quite unusual for his time. Most men in Iran don't spend time in the kitchen but he would often be shopping, cooking, and experimenting with ingredients on weekends.

I have to admit I didn't like everything he made—I can hear my voice saying, "What is this, Baba?" But since I've been away from home, I look back with new appreciation of his cooking flourishes, such as the sesame oil he'd add to a salad. I was suspicious then, but I've since eaten more Asian foods, and I've come to understand and like it.

My baba is a big breakfast person. Often when I call him he's making omelets and I have fond memories of him making this breakfast for me. It's his invention, which is why it's called dadami after the Azeri word for father, but the flavor combination is classic Persian. I'm sure you're going to love it.

PREP TIME: 10 MINS COOK TIME: 10 MINS SERVES: 2

4 eggs
3½ oz (100 g) sheep feta, cut into
   ½ inch (1 cm) cubes
3½ tablespoons (50 g) unsalted butter,
   cut into ½ inch (1 cm) cubes
½ cup (50 g) chopped walnuts
4 teaspoons dried mint
Salt and freshly ground black pepper
4 slices toasted bread of your choice
Nigella seeds, to serve

Bring a saucepan of water to a boil over high heat, add the eggs, then reduce the heat to a simmer and cook for about 10 minutes to hard-boil them. Drain, then run under cold water until cool enough to handle.

Peel the eggs and cut into ½ inch (1 cm) cubes, then transfer to a bowl and add half the feta, the butter, half the walnuts, and the mint. Stir to melt the butter and season to taste with salt and pepper.

Spoon the egg mixture onto the toast and scatter the remaining feta, walnuts, and a few nigella seeds on top.

Enjoy!

Torsh Tareh

HERB OMELET

We love herbs so much in Iran that we not only eat them fresh with every meal, we also cook them, like this green herby stew that's studded with broken just-cooked eggs. Tareh are the garlic chives that are such an important part of the dish and torsh means "sour," which is achieved from verjuice, a tart liquid pressed from unripe grapes. I love the tanginess it brings to this dish. We actually use verjuice a lot: as a seasoning for soups and stews and as a health tonic.

My mom serves this dish with steamed rice but sometimes people have it with bread, too. The eggs aren't supposed to be mixed in: they should be easy to see against the thick green stew.

PREP TIME: 10 MINS **COOK TIME:** 15 MINS **SERVES:** 1

9 oz (250 g) garlic chives, finely chopped

1⅔ cups (50 g) finely chopped flat-leaf parsley, stalks and leaves

¾ cup (45 g) finely chopped dill fronds

1 cup (50 g) finely chopped cilantro, stalks and leaves

¾ cup (50 g) finely chopped spinach

4 garlic cloves, finely chopped

½ teaspoon ground turmeric

1 teaspoon salt

1 teaspoon freshly ground black pepper

2½ tablespoons olive oil

2 eggs

½ cup (125 ml) verjuice

Mint leaves, to serve

Noon Lavash (page 57) or store-bought Persian or Lebanese flatbread, to serve

Place the chopped herbs and spinach, garlic, turmeric, and ½ cup (125 ml) water in a small frying pan over medium heat. Season with the salt and pepper and cook for 5 minutes or until the herbs and spinach have wilted and reduced. Stir in the olive oil.

Whisk the eggs and verjuice in a small bowl, then pour it over the herb mixture and cook for 2 minutes or until the eggs are just set, but still a little runny.

Scatter mint leaves over the herb omelet and serve in the pan with flatbread on the side.

Tompom Omelet

If you head over to the salads chapter, you'll see my tompom salad (page 94), with tomatoes and pomegranate. This is an omelet version of that colorful salad, though without the "pom." Instead, this veggie-packed breakfast has bell pepper, red onion, and cherry tomatoes and is served with sabzi khordan and flatbreads.

This recipe introduces you to my special technique for cooking eggs. Egg whites cook faster than yolks and I really don't like dry, overcooked yolks. So I crack the eggs into the pan, push the yolks to the side, cook the whites with the vegetables, then bring the yolk back in at the end to gently set at the last moment. This method is inspired by soft-boiled eggs: just-set whites and runny yolks.

PREP TIME: 15 MINS COOK TIME: 10 MINS SERVES: 1

2½ tablespoons olive oil
¼ red onion, diced
¼ yellow bell pepper, diced
4 cherry tomatoes, halved
Salt and freshly ground black pepper
2 eggs

TO SERVE
Ground sumac
Noon Lavash (page 57) or store-bought
   Persian or Lebanese flatbread
Sabzi Khordan (page 214)

Heat the olive oil in a small frying pan over medium–high heat, add the onion and bell pepper, and sauté for 5 minutes until golden brown. Add the tomato and cook for 1 minute, then season with salt and pepper.

Push the vegetable mixture to one side of the pan and crack the eggs into the now-empty side of the pan. Using a spoon, gently separate the yolks from the whites. Mix the egg whites into the cooked vegetables and cook for 1 minute, until the egg whites are just set. Spoon the yolks on top of the vegetable mixture, then gently swirl them over the top and briefly cook until they are heated through but still a little runny.

Serve the omelet in the pan or transfer to a plate. Sprinkle a little sumac over the top and serve with flatbread and sabzi khordan on the side.

Feta Omelet (top)
Khakhorma (bottom,
page 32)

Feta Omelet

My father used to make this omelet for me, but I have to admit I didn't like it much when I was younger. Now, in Australia, my tastes have grown up a bit and I love it. I'm not the only one! This is the number-one breakfast in my cafe.

PREP TIME: 5 MINS COOK TIME: 5 MINS SERVES: 1

2½ tablespoons olive oil
2 eggs
3½ oz (100 g) sheep feta, crumbled
Freshly ground black pepper
4 teaspoons nigella seeds
Noon Lavash (page 57) or store-bought
    Persian or Lebanese flatbread, to serve
Sabzi Khordan (page 214), to serve

Heat the olive oil in a small frying pan over low heat. Add the eggs and half the feta, then, using a spoon, gently separate the yolks from the whites and push the yolks to one side of the pan. Stir together the egg whites and feta and cook for 1 minute. Spoon the yolks on top of the cheesy egg white, then gently swirl them over the mixture and briefly cook until they are heated through but still a little runny. Scatter the remaining feta on top and remove from the heat. Season with black pepper.

Either serve the omelet in the pan or transfer to a plate. Scatter the nigella seeds over the top and serve with flatbread and sabzi khordan on the side.

Khakhorma

DATE OMELET

Does a sweet omelet seem strange to you? We love sweets in Iran and people have very warm feelings towards this date omelet (pictured on page 30). They say if you eat it, your day will be good and you will have a lot of energy. Making it is a pleasure because the butter and cinnamon are so fragrant as they cook. I really love eating khakhorma for breakfast but it's also fantastic for lunch or dinner. And even though the omelet has a lot of sweetness from the dates, we still serve it with sabzi khordan.

PREP TIME: 15 MINS COOK TIME: 5 MINS SERVES: 1

1½ tablespoons unsalted butter
5 Persian or 3 Medjool dates, pitted
1 teaspoon ground cinnamon
2 eggs
Noon Lavash (page 57) or store-bought
    Persian or Lebanese flatbread, to serve
Sabzi Khordan (page 214), to serve

Melt the butter in a frying pan over low heat. Add the dates and 2½ tablespoons water and cook for 1 minute until the dates become soft. Lightly mash the dates with a spatula, stir in half the cinnamon, then push the mixture to one side of the pan. Crack the eggs into the now-empty side of the pan and use a spoon to gently separate the yolks from the whites. Gently mix the egg whites into the date mixture and cook for 1 minute, until the egg whites are just set. Spoon the yolks on top, then gently swirl them over the mixture and briefly cook until they are heated through but still a little runny.

Either serve the omelet in the pan or transfer to a plate. Sprinkle the remaining cinnamon over the top and serve with flatbread and sabzi khordan on the side.

Mirza Ghasemi

SMOKED EGGPLANT OMELET

I call this an omelet, but mirza ghasemi is as much about the smoky eggplant as it is about the eggs. It's a very traditional breakfast from the north of Iran, my favorite region. People love it in the morning but it's also eaten for lunch and dinner.

Mirza ghasemi is very popular in my restaurant and I love making it because the garlic and turmeric are fragrant and the flavors are so comforting; it's like putting a hug on a plate for my customers. It also looks so pretty, with streaks of just-cooked yolks and a bright sprinkling of sumac. If you want to make it for brunch, I suggest preparing the eggplant the night before.

PREP TIME: 20 MINS COOK TIME: 25 MINS SERVES: 2

1 eggplant
2½ tablespoons olive oil
1 yellow onion, diced
2 garlic cloves, finely chopped
1 teaspoon ground turmeric
1 tomato, diced
1 teaspoon salt
1 teaspoon freshly ground black pepper
4 eggs

TO SERVE
Ground sumac
Noon Lavash (page 57) or store-bought
    Persian or Lebanese flatbreads
Sabzi Khordan (page 214)

If grilling the eggplant, heat the grill to high heat. Alternatively, use a gas stovetop. Place the eggplant on the grill or over a gas flame and cook, using tongs to turn them frequently, until the skin is charred and blackened and the flesh is tender—this will take about 20 minutes on the grill or about 5 minutes on the stovetop. Transfer the eggplant to a bowl, cover with plastic wrap, and allow to steam for about 10 minutes.

Peel and discard most of the charred eggplant skin along with the stalk. It is okay to leave a few small pieces of skin, as this will enhance the smoky flavor.

Heat the olive oil in a frying pan over high heat, add the onion, and sauté for about 2 minutes until golden brown, then add the garlic and turmeric and cook for 1–2 minutes, until fragrant. Add the tomato, smoky eggplant, salt, and pepper and sauté for 2 minutes. Reduce the heat to low and push the mixture to one side of the pan. Crack the eggs into the now-empty side of the pan and use a spoon to gently separate the yolks from the whites. Gently mix the egg whites through the eggplant mixture and cook for 1 minute. Spoon the yolks on top, then gently swirl them over the mixture and briefly cook until they are heated through but still a little runny.

Serve the omelet in the pan or divide between plates. Sprinkle some sumac over the top and serve with flatbreads and sabzi khordan on the side.

Ghahve Khunee Omelet

STREET-FOOD TOMATO OMELET

I have so many fond memories of this dish. It's traditionally served in shisha shops, the cafes where older men gather to smoke water pipes, drink tea, and solve the problems of the world. Shisha shops don't really serve food but inevitably people get hungry while they're hanging around, so it's become traditional for staff to whip up a quick tomato omelet for customers and serve it with bread, raw red onion, herbs, and lemon. If you want one, all you ask for is "omelet." There's no menu as such.

I left Iran aged 23, long before the "shisha shop age" but, if you promise not to tell my parents, I'll let you in on a secret. When I was in high school in Tehran, I was so naughty. I was in a little gang with three of my friends. We arrived at school at 7 am, then the gate was locked to keep us in. But if we couldn't stand being at school anymore, we would climb the wall at about 10 am and escape. We'd always end up at Amoo Hooshang Cafe where the owner, Uncle Hooshang, would let us puff on a pipe and make us an omelet. I don't know why he was so generous, but I'll never forget his kindness to four cheeky kids.

PREP TIME: 5 MINS COOK TIME: 5 MINS SERVES: 1

2½ tablespoons olive oil
1 tomato, diced
Heaped 1 tablespoon tomato paste
Salt and freshly ground black pepper
2 eggs
Noon Lavash (page 57) or store-bought
    Persian or Lebanese flatbread, to serve
Sabzi Khordan (page 214), to serve

Heat the olive oil in a small frying pan over high heat. Add the tomato and tomato paste and cook, stirring, for 2 minutes. Season with salt and pepper, then reduce the heat to low and push the mixture to one side of the pan. Crack the eggs into the now-empty side of the pan and use a spoon to gently separate the yolks from the whites. Mix the egg whites through the tomato mixture and cook for 1 minute, until the egg whites are just set. Spoon the yolks on top, then gently swirl them over the mixture and briefly cook until they are heated through but still a little runny.

Serve the omelet in the pan or transfer to a plate, and serve with flatbread and sabzi khordan on the side.

Summer Banquet

See over page for dishes

Summer Banquet

Iranians talk a lot about "cold" and "hot" dishes but it has nothing to do with the actual temperature; it's more of a traditional food-as-medicine approach. These are typical summer dishes that my mother would say are good for making you cooler and relaxing you when the sun is beating down.

DALAL DIP
herb salt and yogurt dip
52

ZERESHK POLOW BA MORGH
barberry pilaf with chicken
125

DOLMEH

stuffed vine leaves

55

NOON LAVASH

Persian flatbread

57

ABDOOGH KHIAR

chilled yogurt and cucumber soup

101

KHIAR PANIR

cucumber salad

93

KHAGINEH

sugar pancake

197

Although the word "mezze" comes from the Persian "mazeh" (taste), in Iran we don't really eat dips and snacks in the same way that we do in my adopted country of Australia or elsewhere.

If my aunties and uncles were coming to visit, my parents would first offer tea, then lay out nuts and fruit, both fresh and dried. Younger people do it a bit differently—if I was gathering with my friends (perhaps for some illegal drinking!), we'd snack on walnuts and feta. When it comes to Iranian gatherings, there aren't formal dining courses that we follow.

Instead, larger dishes are slowly added to the food already on the table and the meals slip from one course to the next.

The recipes in this chapter play more into the idea of mezze as a dips and snacks spread, with some recipes that are traditional and others that I've developed since arriving in Melbourne. I've really come to appreciate the Australian passion for dips! In fact, at my restaurant my dips trio is the most popular way my guests start a meal— even the Iranians!

Dips & Snacks

Dadami Dip

This dip is very special to me because it's something my father would make. When I was little, he would travel to the countryside in the north of Iran to visit his sister, my aunty Sara. She lives on a farm and they hardly ever go grocery shopping—they have cows, a big garden, and everything they need, and she makes butter, cheese, yogurt, and labneh.

When my father returned he always brought a huge 44 lb (20 kg) tub of labneh with him. We would eat it with our dinner and have it with bread as a snack, but after a few days we would be sick of it so my father would get creative. Every Iranian eats sabzi khordan (page 214), our famous mixed herb salad. My father took that idea and ran with it: he would chop mint, dill, basil, and red onion, mix in some rose petals and fresh chile, then stir the mixture into the labneh. We would eat it at home and my mother would also put it in a flatbread, which I would take to school to have during breaktime. It brings back a lot of memories.

When I started making this recipe in my cooking classes, it didn't have a name so I called it dadami dip. My father is Azeri (of Azerbaijani descent) and dadami means "daddy" in his language. I think this is my number-one dip recipe.

PREP TIME: 15 MINS + OVERNIGHT IF MAKING LABNEH **SERVES:** 4–5

4½ cups (2 lb 4 oz) plain yogurt
  (or use 1¾ cups/500 g store-bought labneh)
½ bunch mint, leaves roughly chopped
½ bunch dill, fronds roughly chopped
½ bunch basil, leaves roughly chopped
½ red onion, roughly chopped
½ long green chile, roughly chopped
2 teaspoons cumin seeds
2 teaspoons ground sumac
Handful edible dried rose petals
½ cup (125 ml) extra-virgin olive oil
Salt and freshly ground black pepper
Nigella seeds, to serve (optional)

If you want to make your own labneh, spoon the yogurt into a large square of cheesecloth or a clean tea towel. Bring the corners together and tie in a knot to secure the yogurt. Suspend the yogurt bundle over a bowl to catch the whey (making sure that the yogurt doesn't touch the base of the bowl). Set aside to hang in the fridge overnight.

The next day, spoon the labneh into a large bowl and discard the whey. Add the herbs, onion, chile, spices, half the dried rose petals, and half the olive oil and stir to combine. Season to taste with salt and pepper.

Transfer the dadami dip to a serving bowl and scatter the remaining dried rose petals and a few nigella seeds (if using) over the top. Drizzle over the remaining olive oil and serve as part of a mezze spread.

The dip will keep in an airtight container in the fridge for up to 1 week.

Mast Bademjan Dip

EGGPLANT AND YOGURT DIP

In Iran, we eat this eggplant (bademjan) dip as a side dish, especially with lamb. Smokiness is a key feature here so it's important to cook the eggplants over an open flame—you can do this outside on the grill or inside using a gas stovetop. Although the charred eggplant skins are peeled, I don't mind leaving in a few blackened pieces because they add more flavor. The yogurt (mast) and tahini make the dip beautifully creamy and rounded in flavor.

PREP TIME: 15 MINS COOK TIME: 20 MINS SERVES: 4

2 large eggplants
1 cup (260 g) Greek-style yogurt
½ cup (135 g) tahini
2 garlic cloves, crushed to a paste
4 teaspoons ground sumac, plus extra to serve
Salt and freshly ground black pepper
Pomegranate arils and chopped mint leaves,
    to serve (optional)
Olive oil, for drizzling

If grilling the eggplants, heat the grill to high heat. Alternatively, use a gas stovetop. Place the eggplants on the grill or over a gas flame and cook, using tongs to turn them frequently, until the skins are charred and blackened and the flesh is tender—this will take about 20 minutes on the grill or about 5 minutes on the stovetop. Transfer the eggplants to a bowl, cover with plastic wrap, and allow to steam for about 10 minutes.

Peel and discard most of the charred eggplant skins along with the stalks. It's okay to leave a few small pieces of skin, as this will enhance the smoky flavor.

Chop or blend the eggplant flesh, then transfer to a bowl and add the yogurt, tahini, garlic, and sumac. Stir well to combine and season to taste with salt and pepper.

Spoon into a serving bowl and scatter over a little extra sumac, a few pomegranate arils, and some chopped mint, if desired. Drizzle with olive oil and serve as part of a mezze spread or as a side to lamb.

The dip will keep in an airtight container in the fridge for up to 3 days.

Mast Laboo

BEET DIP

Everyone loves this dip but it's not a traditional Persian dish at all! I came up with it when I started running cooking classes and catering because I wanted something bright, tasty, and vegetarian. In my restaurant, I do a trio of dips and it looks so nice to have this beautiful pink-purple dip with its bright-green parsley garnish. It's so good with felafel, too (page 56).

PREP TIME: 10 MINS **COOK TIME:** 20 MINS **SERVES:** 4

2 large beets, peeled and quartered
2 cups (500 g) Greek-style yogurt
1 teaspoon ground nutmeg
1 teaspoon ground sumac
Salt and freshly ground black pepper
Finely chopped flat-leaf parsley, stalks
    and leaves, to serve
Olive oil, for drizzling

Place the beets in a large saucepan and cover with water. Bring to a simmer over high heat and cook the beets for 20 minutes or until soft and easily pierced with a knife. Drain and set aside to cool.

Grate the beets or process in the bowl of a food processor to a chunky paste. Transfer to a large bowl and add the yogurt, nutmeg, and sumac. Stir to combine and season to taste with salt and pepper.

Scatter parsley over the top of the beet dip, along with a drizzle of olive oil, and serve as part of a mezze spread.

The dip will keep in an airtight container in the fridge for up to 3 days.

Savory Feta Truffles

You would never see these feta truffles in Iran, but they bring together some typical Persian flavors in a new form. Feta, fresh herbs, and bread are such a popular combination that they have their own name: noon panir sabzi (bread, cheese, herbs). We also often eat feta with walnuts. In fact, my mother used to mix feta and crushed walnuts in a bowl and we would have it with flatbread for breakfast, along with our black tea. So this recipe brings together the feta–herb and feta–nut combinations in a new dish!

I made this up when I opened my restaurant. You could have it for breakfast, but it's also great as a snack with a glass of wine or served as part of a mezze spread.

PREP TIME: 20 MINS SERVES: 8

1 cup (100 g) walnuts
1 lb 2 oz (500 g) sheep feta, crumbled
1 teaspoon ground fennel seeds
1 cup (20 g) mint leaves, finely chopped
1 cup (30 g) basil leaves, finely chopped
1/3 cup (20 g) finely chopped dill fronds
1/3 cup (40 g) finely chopped garlic chives
Olive oil, for drizzling
Nigella seeds, to serve
Noon Lavash (page 57) or store-bought
   Persian or Lebanese flatbreads, to serve

Place the walnuts in the bowl of a food processer and process for 10 seconds until roughly chopped. Alternatively, you can use a mortar and pestle. Transfer the chopped walnuts to a bowl and add half the feta and half the ground fennel seeds. Stir until well combined, then, using your hands, shape the mixture into walnut-sized truffles.

In a separate bowl, combine the remaining feta and ground fennel seeds with the herbs, then roll into walnut-sized truffles.

Place the two types of truffles together on a serving plate and drizzle with a little olive oil. Sprinkle with nigella seeds and serve with flatbread.

The truffles will keep in an airtight container in the fridge for up to 3 days.

Zeytoon Parvardeh

OLIVE AND WALNUT CHUNKY DIP

*Around the northern Iranian city of Rudbar there are many farmers who grow olives.
I think of it as zeytoon (olive) city, and this recipe always takes me back there.*

*Parvadeh means "marinated" or "preserved," but it also includes the sense of being nourished.
In Iran, we serve this mixture of olives, walnuts, and pomegranate as a side dish, especially with
rice and fish, but in my restaurant I serve it as a chunky dip.*

*Golpar (Heracleum persicum; also known as Persian hogweed or angelica) is an important herb in
Persian cooking and it has a particular fragrant bitterness. It can be purchased dried and ground
from Middle Eastern supermarkets and online, but if you can't find it just leave it out.*

*You can serve this dish as soon as it's made, but it's more delicious to let the flavors meld and
develop for a few days. You can make a big batch and keep it in the fridge for a couple of months.*

PREP TIME: 25 MINS SERVES: 4–5

1 cup (100 g) walnuts
1 cup (250 ml) pomegranate molasses
2 garlic cloves, crushed to a paste
Arils from 1 pomegranate
4 teaspoons dried mint
4 teaspoons olive oil
2½ tablespoons granulated sugar
1 teaspoon salt
1 teaspoon freshly ground black pepper
4 teaspoons ground golpar
   (Persian hogweed; optional)
14 oz (400 g) pitted green or black olives
Chopped flat-leaf parsley leaves, to serve

Place the walnuts in the bowl of a food processor
with ½ cup (125 ml) water and process for
10 minutes, until a paste forms (if the mixture is
dry, add a little more water a tablespoon at a time,
but it should not be runny).

Transfer the walnut paste to a bowl and add
the pomegranate molasses, garlic, half the
pomegranate arils, the mint, olive oil, sugar, salt,
pepper, and golpar (if using). Stir well to combine,
then fold in the olives. Scatter the remaining
pomegranate arils over the top, along with a few
chopped parsley leaves, and serve as part of a
mezze spread.

Hummus

Hummus isn't traditional in Iran but we know it from nearby Arab countries. People have very strong opinions about hummus but, when I started to make it myself, I knew changing the recipe wouldn't scandalize anyone in my family because no one ever ate it. That gave me freedom! So, I added basil to make it taste more like a pesto. I received so much positive feedback that I've kept making it this way.

I prefer to use dried chickpeas, which need to be soaked in water for 24 hours. That said, if I don't get around to soaking them, I'll happily use canned and you can, too.

PREP TIME: 30 MINS + 24 HOURS SOAKING TIME IF USING DRIED CHICKPEAS
COOK TIME: 20–30 MINS IF USING DRIED CHICKPEAS SERVES: 10

2 cups (400 g) dried chickpeas (garbanzo beans), soaked in cold water for 24 hours OR 4 x 14 oz (400 g) cans chickpeas
5 garlic cloves
½ bunch basil leaves
4 teaspoons salt
4 teaspoons freshly ground black pepper
½ cup (125 ml) freshly squeezed lemon juice
1 cup (250 ml) extra-virgin olive oil, plus extra to serve
1 cup (270 g) tahini
Ground sumac, to serve

If using dried chickpeas, drain and rinse the chickpeas, then place them in a large saucepan and cover with about ¾ inches (2 cm) water. Cover with a lid and place over medium heat. Bring to a simmer and cook the chickpeas, straining off the froth that forms on the surface, for 20–30 minutes, until soft. Some chickpeas take longer than others, so keep checking until you're sure they're all cooked. Drain, reserving 1½ cups (375 ml) of the cooking water.

If using canned chickpeas, drain and discard the chickpea liquid from 2 cans, and keep the liquid of the remaining 2.

Place the chickpeas in the large bowl of a food processor along with the chickpea liquid, garlic, basil, salt, pepper, and lemon juice. Process for 15–20 minutes, until completely smooth. Add the olive oil and process for another 2 minutes, then add the tahini and process for 3 minutes.

Transfer the hummus to a serving bowl and sprinkle sumac over the top. Drizzle with olive oil and serve as part of a mezze spread.

The hummus will keep in an airtight container in the fridge for up to 3 days.

Dalal & Dalal Dip

HERB SALT DIP

Iranian dalal is a herb salt that is kept in a jar and sprinkled over cucumbers or sour green plums as a snack. Even as a kid, I loved dalal on cucumbers—maybe it's how my mother got me to eat green vegetables!

In Iran, dalal is made with local herbs, which are stone-ground and mixed with salt to help preserve them. It's a very simple preparation but to me it tastes exactly like home. My version uses easy-to-find herbs. I'm also sharing the recipe for my dalal dip, mixed with the cucumber that it's traditionally sprinkled on.

PREP TIME: 10 MINS SERVES: 4

DALAL
2 bunches mint, leaves roughly chopped
1 bunch cilantro, stalks and leaves
    roughly chopped
1 bunch flat-leaf parsley, stalks and leaves
    roughly chopped
½ bunch basil, leaves roughly chopped
4 garlic cloves, roughly chopped
5 tablespoons (90 g) sea salt flakes

DALAL DIP
2 cups (500 g) Greek-style yogurt
1 Persian or Lebanese cucumber, finely diced
2½ tablespoons Dalal (see above)
Edible dried rose petals, to serve

DALAL
Process the herbs and garlic in a food processor for 10–15 minutes, until finely chopped and well combined. Transfer to a bowl and stir in the salt.

Keep the dalal in a jar in the fridge and sprinkle over salads and cucumbers, or use it to make the delicious dip below. Remember that dalal is a herb salt so it is very salty by itself. Kept in the fridge, the dalal will keep for up to 6 months.

DALAL DIP
Combine the yogurt, cucumber, and dalal in a bowl. Scatter over a few dried rose petals and serve.

The dip will keep in an airtight container in the fridge for up to 3 days.

"A gardener grows flowers and makes the garden beautiful. I cook for humanity and make the world a more beautiful place in that way."

Dolmeh

STUFFED VINE LEAVES

These dolmeh are based on my mother's recipe. I have memories of wrapping her dolmeh in flatbread and enjoying the sweet and sour flavors—a characteristic Persian combination—that came with every bite. You might be surprised to find yellow split peas in these stuffed vine leaves, but in Iran they are just as important as the rice.

Traditionally, Persian dolmeh are filled with ground beef or lamb, but when I taught them at my cooking classes I could see how much people loved the vegetarian version. I also saw the fun they had rolling the dolmeh—it's a great family or group activity.

You can purchase vine leaves in brine from Middle Eastern supermarkets.

PREP TIME: 1 HOUR **COOK TIME:** 35 MINS **MAKES:** 40–50

½ cup (100 g) long-grain basmati rice
½ cup (110 g) yellow split peas
40–50 vine leaves in brine, drained, plus extra leaves for cooking
1 cup (250 ml) olive oil
1 large yellow onion, finely chopped
2 teaspoons ground turmeric
2 teaspoons freshly ground black pepper
½ bunch mint leaves, finely chopped
½ bunch cilantro, stalks and leaves finely chopped
½ bunch flat-leaf parsley, stalks and leaves finely chopped
4 teaspoons dried tarragon (optional)
½ cup (125 ml) pomegranate paste or molasses
2 teaspoons salt
½ cup (125 ml) freshly squeezed lemon juice
5 tablespoons (60 g) granulated sugar

Soak the rice and split peas in a large bowl of cold water for 30 minutes.

Meanwhile, bring a large saucepan of water to a boil, then add the vine leaves, and boil for 5 minutes. Drain and set aside.

Drain the rice and split peas, then transfer to a pot and add 2 cups (500 ml) water. Bring to a boil over high heat and cook for 10–15 minutes, until the rice and split peas are very soft and the water has evaporated. If there is still water in the pot by the time the rice and split peas are cooked, simply drain.

Heat 2½ tablespoons of the olive oil in a large frying pan over high heat. Add the onion and sauté for about 2 minutes, until golden, then stir through the turmeric, pepper, and herbs. Sauté for 5 minutes, then add the cooked rice and split peas and mix well. Remove the pan from the heat, stir in the pomegranate paste or molasses and salt, and set aside to cool.

To make the dolmeh, working with one vine leaf at a time, spine side up, place a heaped tablespoon of the cooled rice and split pea filling along the base of the vine leaf. Roll up the leaf, tucking in the sides as you go, to form a roll. Repeat with the remaining vine leaves and filling.

Line the base of a large nonstick pot with a layer of flattened vine leaves to protect the dolmeh from burning. Arrange the dolmeh over the vine leaves, in layers if necessary, ensuring they are snugly packed together.

Whisk the lemon juice, sugar, and remaining olive oil in a bowl and pour the mixture over the dolmeh. Cook, covered, over medium–low heat for 20 minutes.

Allow the dolmeh to cool to room temperature and serve, or refrigerate once cool and serve cold.

The dolmeh will keep in an airtight container in the fridge for 3–4 days.

Felafel

In every city and town in Iran you'll find felafel shops, at least two or three in each suburb. It's the kind of snack you have a few times a week: cheap, quick, and always accessible. Usually, it's a do-it-yourself kind of system. The owner gives you felafel in pita bread and you add your own pickles, veggies, and sauces.

My version of felafel has been road-tested in my cooking classes and in my cafe. It has more spices than a classic Persian version but everyone seems to love it.

This is one recipe where you do need to plan ahead and soak dried chickpeas, as they form the base of the dish.

PREP TIME: 20 MINS + OVERNIGHT SOAKING TIME COOK TIME: 20 MINS MAKES: ABOUT 40

2 cups (400 g) dried chickpeas,
    soaked in cold water for 24 hours
    (do not use canned)
2 large yellow onions, roughly chopped
½ garlic bulb, cloves peeled
½ bunch cilantro, stalks and leaves
    roughly chopped
½ bunch flat-leaf parsley, stalks and leaves
    roughly chopped
4 teaspoons cumin seeds
4 teaspoons fennel seeds
4 teaspoons dried oregano
2 teaspoons ground turmeric
2 teaspoons freshly ground black pepper
2 teaspoons salt
Vegetable oil, for deep-frying

TO SERVE
Flatbreads
Khiar Shoor (page 184)
Sliced tomato
Shredded lettuce
Hummus (page 50)
Mayonnaise

Drain the chickpeas, then place in a large bowl and add the remaining ingredients except the vegetable oil. Lightly toss to roughly combine, then, working in batches, process the ingredients in a food processor until you have a grainy mixture. You can also use a meat grinder to do this, passing the ingredients separately through the grinder. Transfer to a large bowl.

Heat enough vegetable oil for deep-frying in a large saucepan to 350°F (180°C) or until a pinch of the felafel mixture dropped into the oil turns golden in 10–15 seconds.

Using your hands, two spoons, or a felafel scoop if you have one, form the mixture into about 40 felafel.

Working in batches of 15, carefully lower the felafel into the hot oil and cook for 2–3 minutes or until golden brown. Remove the felafel using a slotted spoon and drain on paper towels.

Serve the felafel with flatbread, khiar shoor, tomato, lettuce, hummus, and mayonnaise.

Noon Lavash

PERSIAN FLATBREAD

We eat bread for breakfast, lunch, and dinner—no meal is complete without it. Flatbread is often used in place of silverware to scoop up food, for wiping our plates clean, and for wrapping anything from cheese to felafel.

There's no such thing as stale bread either! Yesterday's bread is turned into tilit (dried bread that is torn and added to soups and stews to bulk them up) or tahdig (layered bread on the base of a pot of rice that forms a crisp golden crust).

There's a bakery on every street in Iran and most families buy their bread daily. But if you don't have a Persian bakery down the road, you can easily make your own noon (or nan, if you're being more formal).

PREP TIME: 1½ HOURS **COOK TIME:** 40 MINS **MAKES:** 8

2½ tablespoons (24 g) active dried yeast
½ cup (125 ml) warm water
3¾ cups (450 g) all-purpose flour,
    plus extra for dusting
½ cup (125 ml) vegetable oil
2 teaspoons salt

Combine the yeast and warm water in a jug, then cover and set aside for 10 minutes until frothy.

Pour the yeast mixture into a large bowl and add the remaining ingredients along with 1 cup (250 ml) water. Mix with your hands to bring the dough together, then turn out onto a lightly floured work surface and knead for 10 minutes or until you have a very smooth dough.

Divide the dough into eight even-sized portions and roll the portions into balls. Set aside, covered with a clean tea towel, to proof for 40 minutes.

Working with one portion at a time, roll the dough balls out on a lightly floured work surface into 1/16 inch (1 mm) thick circles.

Heat a large frying pan over high heat until very hot, then reduce the heat to low. Add one of the dough circles to the dry pan and cook, pressing the dough gently with a spatula as it puffs up and flipping regularly, for 5 minutes until lightly golden with a few crispy bits. Transfer to a plate and repeat with the remaining dough.

If you would like a crispier bread to serve with dips, cook each side for an extra 2 minutes.

TILIT

To make tilit for Abgoosht (page 156) and Abdoogh Khiar (page 101), cook the bread until very crisp, then leave out overnight, uncovered, to dry out further. We use dried bread for tilit, as it holds up well when soaked in soups and stews.

Winter Banquet

See over page for dishes

Winter Banquet

Yalda Night (winter solstice) is the longest, darkest night of the year. We tend to eat dishes that are warming, soothing, and comforting, typically featuring nuts and spices. I've crafted this menu with that in mind.

FELAFEL

56

KASHK E BADEMJAN
eggplant with kashk

64

ASH SHOLE GHALAMKAR
hearty bean, lamb, and rice soup

106

NOON LAVASH
Persian flatbread

57

ZERESHK POLOW
barberry pilaf

172

TOMPOM SALAD

94

BLISS BALLS

196

To be honest, we don't usually have appetizers in Iran. Unless we have guests, or it's a special occasion, dishes just accumulate on the table and each part of the meal blends into the next. But in a more Western-style meal, all of these dishes work wonderfully as appetizers, sides, or easy weeknight dinners.

I've also included some of my favorite street-food dishes here. Serve them for lunch or dinner for one or as part of a banquet. You can't really go wrong!

Appetizers, Sides & Street Food

Kashk e Bademjan

EGGPLANT WITH KASHK

Out of the dozens of dishes I've made in my cooking classes, this recipe was voted the most popular by the 3,000 people who have come to me over the years. It's simple but the flavors are so delicious. Eggplants are eaten a lot in Northern Iran. Sometimes they're fried, but I personally love flame-cooked eggplant. It has a great smoky flavor plus you don't need any oil.

In this recipe, I pan-fry the eggplant after it's been cooked, just to add a little golden color. The garlic and onion are gently cooked too, taking away their sharpness. Kashk brings its special flavor profile to this dish, but if you can't find it yogurt is fine to use instead.
We serve this as a main dish in Iran but you can also serve it with bread as an appetizer.

PREP TIME: 15 MINS **COOK TIME:** 40 MINS **SERVES:** 4

3 large eggplants
1 cup (250 ml) olive oil
2 large yellow onions, 1 finely diced, 1 thinly sliced
6 garlic cloves, finely chopped
2 teaspoons ground turmeric
2 teaspoons freshly ground black pepper
4 tablespoons dried mint
2 teaspoons salt
Generous ¾ cup (200 ml) liquid kashk (or plain yogurt), plus extra to serve
Chopped walnuts, to serve

If grilling the eggplants, heat the grill to high heat. Alternatively, use a gas stovetop. Place the eggplants on the grill or over a gas flame and cook, using tongs to turn them frequently, until the skins are charred and blackened and the flesh is tender—this will take about 20 minutes on the grill or about 5 minutes on the stovetop. Transfer the eggplants to a bowl, cover with plastic wrap, and allow to steam for about 10 minutes.

Peel and discard most of the charred eggplant skins along with the stalks. It is okay to leave a few small pieces of skin, as this will enhance the smoky flavor.

Heat ½ cup (125 ml) of the olive oil in a frying pan over medium heat, add the diced onion, and cook for 5 minutes until golden. Add the garlic, turmeric, and pepper and sauté for 2 minutes. Add 2 tablespoons of the dried mint and cook for 1 minute, then add the eggplant and cook for 5 minutes or until lightly golden. Remove the pan from the heat and stir in the salt and kashk.

Heat 4 tablespoons of the remaining oil in a small frying pan over high heat. Add the sliced onion and sauté for 5 minutes or until dark brown. Transfer to a plate. Add the remaining oil, along with the remaining dried mint, to the pan. Fry the mint for 15–20 seconds, then remove from the heat.

Transfer the eggplant mixture to a serving plate and top with the fried onion, fried mint, and chopped walnuts. Drizzle with extra kashk and serve.

Kotlets

PERSIAN BURGERS

I'll start with a sad food story and then tell you why I love this Persian version of a hamburger patty! Every man in Iran has to go into the army for 18 months to two years. When I did my compulsory training, every Monday was kotlet day. And the kotlets were awful! I'm not sure if it was the meat or the way they cooked them but they were grey and dry and almost—almost!— ruined the memory of my mother's kotlets.

When I came out of the army, I had to recover the kotlet's reputation by eating a lot of my mom's delicious version. And this is that recipe. I love it. Western-style burgers are fine but it's so nice to mix ground meat with potatoes, onion, and spices. It's a burger but extra!

You can eat kotlets with rice, bread, and fresh tomatoes or you can make a wrap with khiar shoor (page 184), tomato, lettuce, and mayonnaise. Usually, we make it with lamb or beef (or a mixture of the two), but chicken is a good alternative.

PREP TIME: 20 MINS **COOK TIME:** 20 MINS **SERVES:** 4–5

1 lb 2 oz (500 g) ground beef or lamb
  (or use ground chicken)
2 potatoes, peeled and grated
3 garlic cloves, grated
1 yellow onion, grated
2 teaspoons ground turmeric
2 teaspoons salt
2 teaspoons freshly ground black pepper
½ cup (125 ml) vegetable oil

TO SERVE
Sliced tomato
Sliced cucumber
French fries

Combine all of the ingredients except the oil in a large bowl and, using your hands, mix thoroughly until well combined.

Take a fistful of the mixture and shape it into a burger patty. Set aside on a tray and repeat to make 10 patties.

Heat the oil in a frying pan over medium heat. Working in batches, add the burger patties and cook for 5 minutes on each side or until cooked through to your liking.

Serve the kotlets with sliced tomato and cucumber and a side of hot fries.

Kuku Sabzi

HERB FRITTATA

Kuku is like a frittata and we have many versions in Iran. I like to serve it sabzi (herb) style at SalamaTea and it is very popular. It's a very traditional dish but I've changed it a bit, adding potatoes to soften the intensity of the herbs, and dried barberries because I love their tart bite, plus they look great, too.

I've also developed a vegan version, using the starchiness of raw potatoes to bind the ingredients. After grating the uncooked potatoes, squeeze the liquid from them using a clean tea towel before mixing with the cooked potatoes and other ingredients.

PREP TIME: 20 MINS **COOK TIME: 30 MINS SERVES: 4**

1 large potato, peeled
1 small yellow onion, grated (optional)
9 oz (250 g) chopped garlic chives
1¼ cups (65 g) chopped cilantro,
　　stalks and leaves
1¼ cups (35 g) chopped flat-leaf parsley,
　　stalks and leaves
4 garlic cloves, finely chopped
4 eggs, lightly beaten (optional; omit if vegan)
2 teaspoons ground turmeric
Salt and freshly ground black pepper
½ cup (125 ml) olive oil
½ cup (35 g) dried barberries (optional)
½ cup (50 g) chopped walnuts (optional)

Grate one-third of the potato and set aside on a clean tea towel. Roughly chop the remaining potato, then place in a saucepan, cover with cold water, and season well with salt. Bring to a boil over high heat, then reduce the heat to a simmer and cook the potato for 8–10 minutes, until soft. Drain and place in a large bowl.

Add the onion (if using) to the grated potato, then roll up in the tea towel and wring it out to remove the excess liquid. Add the dried grated potato and onion to the cooked potato, along with the herbs, garlic, egg (if using), and turmeric. Season with salt and pepper to taste and mix really well.

Heat the olive oil in an 8 inch (20 cm) frying pan over low heat. Add half the potato and herb mixture and top with the barberries and walnuts (if using). Spoon the remaining potato and herb mixture over the top, then cover with a lid, and cook for 10 minutes. Carefully flip the frittata onto a plate or wooden board, then slide it back into the pan, uncooked side down. Continue to cook, this time uncovered, for a further 10 minutes until golden.

Slice the kuku sabzi like you would a pizza and enjoy hot or cold. It's also very tasty wrapped in Persian flatbread with sliced tomato.

Kuku Sibzamini

POTATO AND EGG PATTIES

This dish is like a cross between a potato frittata and hash browns. It's really simple to make and a very common snack for kids in Iran. Every time my mother made it, she would make double or triple whatever she thought she needed for the family table because my brother and I would steal pieces of it while she was cooking. One day she went to serve it and the plate was completely empty! Sometimes I'd take my mother's kuku to school, wrapped in flatbread with tomatoes and cucumber pickles.

PREP TIME: 20 MINS **COOK TIME:** 20 MINS **MAKES:** ABOUT 12

1 lb 5 oz (600 g) potatoes, peeled
1 small yellow onion, grated (optional)
4 eggs, lightly beaten (optional; omit if vegan)
2 teaspoons ground turmeric
Salt and freshly ground black pepper
½ cup (125 ml) olive oil

TO SERVE (OPTIONAL)
Noon Lavash (page 57) or store-bought
    Persian or Lebanese flatbreads
Sliced tomato
Sliced cucumber
Sliced Khiar Shoor (page 184) or store-bought
    cucumber pickles

Grate one-third of the potatoes and set aside on a clean tea towel. Roughly chop the remaining potato, then place in a pot, cover with cold water, and season well with salt. Bring to a boil over high heat, then reduce the heat to a simmer and cook the potato for 8–10 minutes, until soft. Drain and place in a large bowl.

Add the onion (if using) to the grated potato, then roll up in the tea towel and wring it out to remove the excess liquid. Add the dried grated potato and onion to the cooked potato, along with the egg (if using) and turmeric. Season with salt and pepper to taste and mix really well.

Take a heaped tablespoon of the mixture and shape it into a patty. Transfer to a tray and repeat with the remaining potato mixture to make about 12 patties.

Heat the oil in a frying pan over medium heat. Working in two batches, add the patties and cook for 4 minutes on each side until golden brown and cooked through.

Serve the patties on their own as a snack or wrap in flatbreads with sliced tomato, sliced cucumber, and khiar shoor for a hearty lunch.

Sambooseh

POTATO SAMOSAS

I can never get enough of these fried potato parcels, served with tomato relish, and I'm confident you will feel the same. The further south you travel in Iran, the closer you get to the Pakistani border and the more you find dishes and spices that we tend to think of as subcontinental. Every mile, it seems they add an extra pinch of chile!

Sambooseh are a popular street food and you see all kinds of meat and vegetable versions. I love them because you can add all sorts of fillings, but this spicy potato version is my favorite.

You might think you need pastry to wrap the filling but you can also use flatbreads or even tortillas, so long as you secure them with toothpicks before frying.

PREP TIME: 50 MINS **COOK TIME:** 45 MINS **SERVES:** 8

4 potatoes, scrubbed
½ cup (125 ml) olive oil
1 large yellow onion, diced
2 teaspoons ground turmeric
2 teaspoons chile powder
2 teaspoons freshly ground black pepper
2 teaspoons salt
½ bunch cilantro, stalks and
  leaves chopped
4 Noon Lavash (page 57) or store-bought Persian
  flatbreads, cut lengthways into 16 x 4 inch
  (40 x 10 cm) strips
Vegetable oil, for deep-frying

TOMATO RELISH
⅓ cup (80 ml) olive oil
1 yellow onion, finely diced
1 garlic clove, finely chopped
2 teaspoons freshly ground black pepper
1 teaspoon ground nutmeg
2½ tablespoons tomato paste
½ cup (85 g) golden raisins
4 large tomatoes, diced
5 tablespoons (60 g) raw sugar
2 teaspoons salt
½ cup (35 g) dried barberries (optional)
½ cup (125 ml) apple cider vinegar

Place the potatoes in a large pot, cover with cold water, and season with salt. Bring to a boil over high heat, then reduce the heat to a simmer and cook the potatoes for 20–30 minutes, until easily pierced with a knife. Drain and peel the potatoes when cool enough to handle and dice into ½ inch (1 cm) pieces.

Meanwhile, to make the tomato relish, heat the oil in a frying pan over high heat. Add the onion and garlic and cook for about 2 minutes, until lightly golden. Add the pepper, nutmeg, and tomato paste and cook for 2 minutes, then add the raisins, tomato, sugar, salt, and barberries (if using). Cook, stirring and mashing frequently, for 10 minutes, until reduced and thick. Stir in the vinegar, then spoon into a bowl and set aside in the fridge.

Heat the oil in a frying pan over high heat, add the onion, and cook for about 2 minutes, until golden. Add the spices and salt, and cook, stirring, for 1 minute. Add the cilantro and cook for another 10 seconds, then transfer the mixture to a large bowl, add the potato, and mash lightly to combine.

Place 2½ tablespoons of the potato mixture at one end of a strip of lavash. Bring the bottom corner up over the top, creating a triangle (or cone shape) over the filling. Fold the triangle over, then down again and continue folding like this until you reach the end of the strip. Tuck any leftover bread into the parcel and secure with toothpicks. Repeat with the remaining filling and lavash strips.

Heat enough oil for deep-frying in a large pot to 350°F (180°C). Working in batches, deep-fry the sambooseh, turning occasionally, for 2–4 minutes, until cooked through and golden. You can also shallow-fry the sambooseh in a large frying pan with ¾ inch (2 cm) oil over medium–high heat. Cook, turning occasionally, for 2–4 minutes. Drain on paper towels. Serve the sambooseh warm with the tomato relish on the side for dipping.

Sosis Bandari

PERSIAN HOTDOGS

I'm going to make a huge statement: Iranian fast food is the best in the world. Don't believe me? Well, don't come at me until you've been there and tried it for yourself!

In the meantime, start your conversion by trying this classic hot-dog sandwich. Originally best known in Southern Iran, it is now found throughout the country, even in school cafeterias. I remember eating it with my friends and it always made my school day better.

Persian hotdogs are available from Middle Eastern supermarkets but any sausage is fine to use in this recipe.

PREP TIME: 20 MINS **COOK TIME:** 15 MINS **SERVES:** 4

½ cup (125 ml) olive oil
1 large yellow onion, sliced
1 teaspoon ground turmeric
1 large potato, scrubbed and cut into small cubes
4 Persian hot-dog sausages (or your favorite hot dog sausages), sliced
2 cups (180 g) sliced mushrooms
2 long red chiles, finely chopped
⅓ cup (90 g) tomato paste
1 teaspoon salt
1 teaspoon freshly ground black pepper

TO SERVE
Mayonnaise
4 hot-dog rolls, sliced open
Shredded lettuce
Sliced tomato
Sliced Khiar Shoor (page 184) or store-bought cucumber pickles

Heat the olive oil in a large frying pan over high heat. Add the onion and cook for 2 minutes, then add the turmeric and potato and cook for 3 minutes until the potato is lightly browned. Add the sliced sausage and mushrooms and continue to cook for 5 minutes, until the sausage is browned. Next, add the chile, tomato paste, salt, and pepper and stir to combine. Cook for a final 2 minutes or until the potato is cooked through, then remove from the heat.

To assemble the hot dogs, spread mayonnaise on the top cut side of each roll. Layer the base of the rolls with lettuce, tomato, and pickles, then divide the sosis bandari among the rolls. Sandwich shut and enjoy. My mouth is watering now!

Dolmeh Bademjan

STUFFED VEGETABLES

"Dolmeh" is the word we use for anything stuffed, and this recipe works with eggplants, bell peppers, large tomatoes, and zucchini. My mom usually made it with eggplant because everyone in our family is a huge fan of this big glossy vegetable, which is also very cheap in Iran. She'd use a mixture of ground lamb and beef, but it's easy to make a vegetarian version by using finely chopped mushrooms instead. If you're stuffing tomatoes, make sure they are large and very firm. Soft tomatoes will collapse into mush!

PREP TIME: 40 MINS **COOK TIME:** 1 HOUR **SERVES:** 4–6

2 red, green, or yellow bell peppers
4 large hard tomatoes
2 eggplants, sliced lengthways in half
2 zucchini, sliced lengthways in half

VEGETABLE STUFFING
½ cup (100 g) long-grain basmati rice, soaked in
    cold water for 30 minutes
½ cup (100 g) yellow split peas, soaked in cold
    water for 30 minutes
1 cup (250 ml) olive oil
2 large yellow onions, diced
2 teaspoons ground turmeric
2 teaspoons freshly ground black pepper
½ bunch mint, leaves picked and finely chopped
½ bunch cilantro, stalks and leaves
    finely chopped
½ bunch flat-leaf parsley, stalks and leaves
    finely chopped
4 teaspoons dried tarragon (optional)
7 oz (200 g) ground lamb and beef (or
    use finely chopped white mushrooms for a
    vegetarian version)
½ cup (125 ml) pomegranate molasses
2 teaspoons salt

To make the vegetable stuffing, drain the rice and yellow split peas, then place in a saucepan and cover with 2 cups (500 ml) cold water. Bring to a boil, then reduce the heat to a simmer and cook for about 15 minutes, until the rice and split peas are very soft. Drain if necessary.

Slice the tops off the bell peppers and tomatoes, setting the tops aside. Hollow out the seeds and membranes from the bell peppers and discard. Using a spoon, scoop out most of the flesh from the remaining vegetables, leaving a ½ inch (1 cm) border. Finely chop the vegetable flesh.

Heat ½ cup (125 ml) of the olive oil in a large frying pan over high heat. Add the onion and cook for about 2 minutes until golden, then add the turmeric, pepper, and herbs and stir to combine. Add the lamb and beef (or mushrooms), along with the reserved vegetable flesh and cook, stirring frequently, for about 15 minutes, until the mixture is cooked through and dry. Add the rice and yellow split peas and cook for 5 minutes, then remove from the heat and stir in the pomegranate molasses and salt until completely incorporated.

Divide the mixture evenly among the hollowed-out vegetables and put the tops back on the bell peppers and tomatoes. Arrange the dolmeh in a large stockpot in a single layer (use two pots if necessary) and pour in 1 cup (250 ml) water and the remaining olive oil. Set over medium–low heat, cover, and cook for 30 minutes or until the vegetables are soft.

Alternatively, to cook the dolmeh in the oven: Preheat it to 400°F (200°C). Arrange the vegetables in a single layer in a roasting pan. Pour in the water and olive oil, cover with foil, and cook for 30–40 minutes, until the vegetables are soft.

Enjoy!

Halim Bademjan

LAMB, LENTILS, AND EGGPLANTS

If I say "lamb and eggplant porridge" you might find the idea a bit strange, but you'll need to trust me on this one! Lamb and eggplant are a great combination (think Greek moussaka), as are lamb and mint (think of an English roast lamb). Add some Persian spices and the tart kick of kashk and I hope I've convinced you to try this delicious, comforting dish.

We usually eat halim bademjan with bread as a main course but it's very rich so I've reduced the quantities and put it here. Serve with bread or tilit (page 57).

PREP TIME: 30 MINS **COOK TIME:** 2 HOURS **SERVES:** 4

1 cup (215 g) dried green lentils
1 lb 9 oz (700 g) lamb neck
3 yellow onions, peeled
3 eggplants
1 cup (250 ml) olive oil
1 teaspoon ground turmeric
6 garlic cloves, roughly chopped
2 teaspoons salt
2 teaspoons freshly ground black pepper
½ cup (15 g) dried mint
1 cup (250 ml) liquid kashk (or use plain yogurt)
¼ cup (30 g) chopped walnuts
Bread of your choice, to serve

Cook the lentils in a saucepan of simmering water for 20–30 minutes, until soft and cooked through. Drain and set aside.

Place the lamb neck and one of the peeled onions in a large pot and cover with 8½ cups (2 liters) water. Bring to a simmer over medium heat and cook for 1 hour 40 minutes or until tender.

Meanwhile, prepare the eggplants. If grilling the eggplants, heat the grill to high heat. Alternatively, use a gas stovetop. Place the eggplants on the grill or over a gas flame and cook, using tongs to turn them frequently, until the skins are charred and blackened and the flesh is tender—this will take about 20 minutes on the grill or about 5 minutes on the stovetop. Transfer the eggplants to a bowl, cover with plastic wrap and allow to steam for about 10 minutes.

Peel and discard most of the charred skins along with the eggplant stalks. It is okay to leave a few small pieces of skin, as this will enhance the smoky flavor. Chop the eggplant.

Dice one of the remaining onions. Heat ½ cup (125 ml) of the olive oil in a frying pan over high heat. Add the onion and cook for 5 minutes or until golden brown. Add the turmeric and garlic and stir for 30 seconds, then remove from the heat. Add the eggplant and lentils and stir to combine.

When the lamb neck is cooked through, drain (reserving the cooking liquid) and set aside until cool enough to handle. Discard the onion. Return the cooking liquid to the pot and simmer over medium heat for 10 minutes or until reduced.

Separate the meat from the bones and shred the lamb using two forks. Add the shredded lamb to the onion and eggplant mixture and season with the salt and pepper. Mix everything together very well, then, using a potato masher, mash the mixture, adding some of the reduced cooking liquid, if necessary, to create a porridge consistency. Transfer to a serving dish.

Slice the remaining onion. Heat the remaining oil in a frying pan over high heat. Add the onion and cook, stirring frequently, for 5 minutes until the onion is golden brown. Stir through the dried mint and remove from the heat.

Spoon the liquid kashk over the lamb and eggplant porridge and top with the fried onion and mint mixture and chopped walnuts. Enjoy with bread.

Jaghur Baghur

LAMB OFFAL FRY-UP

In Iran, offal is very popular, especially lamb's heart and liver, and there are vendors who specialize in this kind of meat, commonly sizzling up barbecued hearts, livers, and kidneys on skewers. The liver is considered a very special delicacy.

This is a homemade pan-seared version that my father used to make at least once a month for our family. Even if you don't think you're an offal lover, I bet you will be after you try this dish.

PREP TIME: 20 MINS COOK TIME: 40 MINS SERVES: 4

1 lamb's heart, cut into 1¼ inch (3 cm) cubes
1 lamb's liver, cut into 1¼ inch (3 cm) cubes
1¼ cups (310 ml) olive oil
3 large yellow onions, diced
2 teaspoons ground turmeric
4 tomatoes, diced
2 hot green chiles, finely chopped
1 garlic clove, finely chopped
2 teaspoons salt
2 teaspoons freshly ground black pepper
2 large potatoes, cut into ½ inch (1 cm) cubes

TO SERVE
½ cup (35 g) dried barberries
Finely chopped flat-leaf parsley, stalks and leaves
Freshly squeezed lemon juice (optional)
Noon Lavash (page 57) or store-bought
   Persian or Lebanese flatbreads

Separately soak the lamb's heart and liver in cold water for 10 minutes, to remove any blood and impurities. Drain and set aside.

Meanwhile, heat ½ cup (125 ml) of the olive oil in a large frying pan over high heat. Add the onion and cook for about 5 minutes, until golden, then add 1 teaspoon of the turmeric and cook, stirring, for 1 minute. Reduce the heat to medium, add the lamb's heart, and cook, stirring frequently, for 10 minutes, then add the lamb's liver and cook for 5 minutes. Stir in the tomato, chile, garlic, salt, and pepper and cook for 5 minutes, until the mixture is dry.

While the offal is cooking, heat ½ cup (125 ml) of the remaining oil in a large frying pan over medium heat. Add the potato and sauté for 5 minutes until it is half cooked. Stir in the remaining turmeric and continue to cook for 5 minutes, until the potato is tender and golden.

Add the potato to the offal mixture and stir well to combine. Remove from the heat and transfer to a serving dish.

Heat the remaining oil in a frying pan over medium heat. Add the dried barberries and cook, stirring, for 1 minute. Scatter the barberries over the offal fry-up and top with the parsley and a squeeze of lemon juice (if using). Serve with flatbreads on the side.

Kuku Adas

LENTIL PATTIES

This is a different kind of kuku, which turns out more like a patty and can be served as a vegetarian burger. This is a real family dish for me; you won't see these patties in many places in Iran but my mother would make them often. I like them because they're very simple—you probably always have the ingredients in your pantry—and it's healthy and filling, too.

PREP TIME: 20 MINS + 40 MINS RESTING TIME **COOK TIME:** 1 HOUR **MAKES:** 15–20

1 cup (215 g) dried green lentils
1 large yellow onion, grated
3 garlic cloves, grated
1 cup (30 g) chopped flat-leaf parsley,
  stalks and leaves
1 egg
½ teaspoon ground turmeric
½ teaspoon freshly ground black pepper
2 teaspoons salt
½ cup (125 ml) olive oil

Cook the lentils in a saucepan of simmering water for 20–30 minutes, until soft and cooked through. Drain, then transfer to a bowl and leave to cool to room temperature. Add the remaining ingredients except the olive oil and mix well, then transfer to a food processor and pulse until the mixture is a mashed consistency, but still a little chunky. Return to the bowl and let the mixture rest for 40 minutes.

Take a fistful of the mixture and shape it into a patty. Transfer to a tray and repeat with the remaining lentil mixture to make 15–20 patties.

Heat the olive oil in a large frying pan over medium heat. Working in batches, cook the lentil patties for 4 minutes on each side until cooked through and golden.

Serve the patties on their own or in burger buns, adding whatever extras you like to make the perfect veggie burgers.

Pooreh Sibzamini

PERSIAN MASH

Everyone loves mashed potatoes so I'm excited to share my Persian version of this classic recipe. It's easy and tasty, and is actually one of the dishes that gave me the confidence to pursue a cooking career in Australia.

In my early years in Melbourne, I volunteered at the Asylum Seeker Resource Center. We had a lot of potatoes to use up and I had the idea to make this dish. It was so popular and it made me really happy to see everyone enjoying it. At the same time, it always makes me think of home—it was my favorite dish as a child—so in a way, these mashed potatoes are a delicious bridge between my old life in Iran and my new life in Australia.

PREP TIME: 10 MINS COOK TIME: 30 MINS SERVES: 4

4 potatoes, scrubbed
7 tablespoons (100 g) unsalted butter
1 teaspoon ground turmeric
1 teaspoon freshly ground black pepper
Salt
1 cup (30 g) chopped flat-leaf parsley, stalks and leaves

Place the potatoes in a large pot, cover with cold water, and season generously with salt. Bring to a boil over high heat, then reduce the heat to a simmer and cook for 20–30 minutes, until a knife slips easily through the potatoes.

Drain the potatoes and set aside until cool enough to handle, then peel. Transfer to a large bowl.

Melt the butter in a frying pan over medium heat. Add the turmeric and cook, stirring, for 20 seconds, then remove from the heat. Stir in the pepper.

Add the melted butter mixture to the potatoes and mashed everything together until really well combined and the potato is smooth. Season to taste with salt, then transfer to a serving dish, top with the parsley, and serve.

Street-Food Feast

These are the dishes you'll find on the streets of Iran, but they also work brilliantly for fun, casual gatherings at home with friends. Get ready for a party!

OLOVIEH
chopped potato salad
96

NOON LAVASH
Persian flatbread
57

SOSIS BANDARI
Persian hotdogs
75

SAMBOOSEH
potato samosas
72

GHAHVE KHUNEE OMELET
street-food tomato omelet
34

SABZI KHORDAN
herb platter
214

ABGOOSHT
lamb shank and chickpea hotpot
156

ASH RESHTEH
noodle soup
102

BASTANI SONNATI
Persian ice cream
198

We don't eat a lot of salads in Iran. We tend to garnish cooked dishes with a lot of fresh herbs and our herb platter, sabzi khordan (page 214), is an essential part of almost every meal. That said, because Iranian cooking is so seasonal, when vegetables are abundant and in season, we eat them every which way we can.

I'm sharing a couple of Persian classics here, plus two of my own salad creations that use Iranian flavors in novel ways.

Salads

Shirazi Salad

Everyone in Iran knows this salad, named after Shiraz, a southern city near the Persian Gulf. The ingredients are very simple; the art is all in the chopping. It's important to cut the cubes very small and very evenly and, for that reason, all the ingredients have to be crisp and firm. The dressing is nice and tart with the great combination of dried mint and sumac.

Shirazi salad is usually made just before serving, but the leftovers are actually really nice because the flavors all meld and the liquid from the vegetables adds to the dressing. The salad dressing recipe makes a lot, and it's traditional to drink the dressing at the end of the meal.

We serve Shirazi salad with pilafs and lamb dishes, such as ghormeh sabzi (page 133) or gheymeh bademjan (page 130).

PREP TIME: 20 MINS SERVES: 4

3 large tomatoes, cut into small cubes
3 Persian or Lebanese cucumbers,
     cut into small cubes
1 large red onion, cut into small cubes
Pomegranate arils, to serve

SHIRAZI SALAD DRESSING
1 cup (250 ml) verjuice or freshly squeezed
     lemon juice
½ cup (125 ml) olive oil
1 teaspoon salt
1 teaspoon freshly ground black pepper
2 teaspoons dried mint
1 teaspoon ground sumac

To make the Shirazi salad dressing, combine the ingredients in a small bowl or jar and whisk or shake to combine.

Arrange the tomato, cucumber, and red onion in a serving bowl, pour over the salad dressing, and toss through. Scatter pomegranate arils over the top and serve.

Khiar Panir

CUCUMBER SALAD

This is a recipe I created for my cooking classes, based on the tried-and-true combination of cucumber and feta. The trick to this dish is to buy firm Persian or Lebanese cucumbers and use a vegetable peeler to shave them into nice long ribbons. The wet crunch of cucumbers and the dry bite of toasted almonds works so well together. I also love the way it looks: the bright greens of the cucumber and parsley contrast so beautifully with the white of the cheese and the bright red of the pomegranate.

PREP TIME: 15 MINS SERVES: 6

8 Persian or Lebanese cucumbers
9 oz (250 g) sheep feta, crumbled
½ bunch flat-leaf parsley, stalks and leaves roughly chopped
Generous 1 cup (95 g) sliced almonds, toasted
Juice of 1 lemon
4 teaspoons olive oil
Salt and freshly ground black pepper
Arils from 1 pomegranate
2 teaspoons nigella seeds

Using a vegetable peeler, shave the cucumbers lengthways, working your way around each cucumber and stopping once you reach the seeds. Place the cucumber ribbons in a bowl and discard the cucumber cores. Add half the feta, half the parsley, and half the almonds and toss to combine, then pour in the lemon juice and olive oil, season with salt and pepper, and toss again.

Scatter the remaining feta, parsley, and almonds over the salad and finish with the pomegranate arils and nigella seeds. Serve immediately.

Tompom Salad

This is another salad I created for my cooking classes. It's based on Iranian flavors but I had the good fortune to work with beloved cookbook author Julia "Ostro" Busuttil Nishimura and we worked on this recipe together.

Pomegranates are extremely popular in Iran. They go in salads, soups, dips, desserts ... you could spend all day eating this colorful fruit. The secret is knowing how to extract the seeds (I cut the pomegranate into quarters and firmly tap the skin with the back of a spoon until the seeds fall out) and how to balance their unique flavor with other elements. Tomatoes and bell pepper are very well loved, too, so this salad takes those three key ingredients and turns them into a dish so beautiful it looks like a work of art. I promise there will be lots of "oohs" and "wows" when you put this dish on the table!

PREP TIME: 15 MINS **SERVES:** 6

⅔ cup (100 g) red cherry tomatoes, quartered
⅔ cup (100 g) yellow cherry tomatoes, quartered
3½ oz (100 g) tiger or plum tomatoes, cut into ¼ inch (5 mm) cubes
2 ripe tomatoes, cut into ¼ inch (5 mm) cubes
1 red bell pepper, cut into ¼ inch (5 mm) cubes
1 small red onion, finely diced
1 garlic clove, crushed
½ teaspoon ground allspice
2 teaspoons white wine vinegar
2 tablespoons pomegranate molasses
¼ cup (60 ml) olive oil, plus extra for drizzling
Salt and freshly ground black pepper
Arils from 1 pomegranate
4 teaspoons small oregano leaves

Place the tomatoes, bell pepper, and onion in a large bowl.

Place the garlic, allspice, white wine vinegar, pomegranate molasses, and olive oil in a small bowl and whisk until well combined. Season to taste with salt and pepper. Pour the dressing over the tomato mixture and gently toss to combine.

Arrange the tomato salad and the juices from the bowl on a large serving plate. Scatter the pomegranate arils and oregano leaves over the top and finish with an extra drizzle of olive oil.

Olovieh

CHOPPED POTATO SALAD

You could think of this classic potato salad as the Persian version of a Russian salad, with meat, pickles, boiled eggs, and vegetables bound in a mayonnaise dressing. The meat we use is a kind of chicken mortadella, which is very popular in Iran, but you could use any kind of cooked chicken sausage or smoked cured sausage.

In Iran, you see this salad in sandwich shops because we often eat it in sandwiches—yes, we love carb on carb where I come from! The most important tip to making this the authentic way is to ensure that all of the ingredients are cut the same size.

This salad is very tasty but it ends up looking quite plain so I always brighten it up with a garnish of chopped parsley, green chile, or chile flakes or a combination of the three.

PREP TIME: 20 MINS COOK TIME: 40 MINS SERVES: 4

1 lb 2 oz (500 g) chicken breast
1 yellow onion, halved
2½ tablespoons salt
4 teaspoons freshly ground black pepper
4 small potatoes, scrubbed
4 eggs
10 Khiar Shoor (page 184), cut into
 ¾ inch (2 cm) cubes
7 oz (200 g) chicken salami (or chicken mortadella
 or other smoked cured sausage), cut into
 ¾ inch (2 cm) cubes (optional)
2½ tablespoons freshly squeezed lemon juice
1 cup (235 g) mayonnaise
Chile flakes, finely chopped long green chile, or
 finely chopped flat-leaf parsley (or a
 combination), to serve

Place the chicken, onion, 4 teaspoons of the salt, and 2 teaspoons of the pepper in a small saucepan. Cover the chicken with water, then place over medium heat, cover, and bring to a boil. Reduce the heat to a simmer and cook the chicken for 30 minutes or until soft and cooked through.

Drain the chicken (discarding the onion) and set aside to cool, then cut into ¾ inch (2 cm) cubes and place in a large bowl.

Meanwhile, place the potatoes and 2 teaspoons of the remaining salt in another saucepan and cover with water. Bring to a boil over medium–high heat, then reduce the heat to a simmer and cook for 15 minutes. Add the eggs and cook for a further 10 minutes until the potatoes are cooked through. Drain and rinse, then peel the potatoes and eggs and cut into ¾ inch (2 cm) cubes. Add to the bowl with the cubed chicken, then add the khiar shoor and chicken salami (if using) and toss the ingredients together.

Combine the lemon juice, mayonnaise, and the remaining ½ tablespoon of salt and 2 teaspoons pepper in a small bowl, then pour the dressing over the salad and toss to combine.

Serve with your choice of chile flakes, chopped green chile, or parsley (or a mixture of all three) scattered over the top. This is a heavy salad, rich in protein and carbs.

Soup (ash) is central to Persian cooking, so much so that the word for "chef" or "cook" is "ash-paz" or "soup maker." And where does such a person work? The words for kitchen is "ash-paz khaneh" or "soup-making home." So if the kitchen is the heart of the home, soup is at the heart of the kitchen.

Soups are eaten at any time of day and at every occasion. They are made and shared to mark personal milestones, from a neighborly welcome to a funeral, an imminent journey or even a baby's first tooth. They're given as nazri (an offering) to community members in need or to mark the anniversary of a death. And the king of soups, ash reshteh (page 102) is always made and eaten for Nowruz (New Year).

Persian soups are usually sturdy, hearty, and nourishing, made with pulses, grains, and sometimes a little meat and vegetables. Most of them are easily a complete meal in themselves. Even though our soups are hearty, they are always carefully balanced with acidic ingredients, such as kashk, verjuice, yogurt, or lemon. And herbs, always herbs!

Soups

Abdoogh Khiar

CHILLED YOGURT AND CUCUMBER SOUP

Every hot day, I can't help but crave this ice-cold soup made with yogurt, cucumber, and herbs. In summer in Iran, I would eat it at least once a week. With the addition of dried fruit, fresh green apples, and walnuts, and made extra cold with ice cubes, it's light and fresh and always looks so pretty with its colorful garnishes.

The soup can also be thickened with bread. When we soak bread in a thin soup and let it soak up the juices to help bulk it up, we call it "tilit." If you want to turn abdoogh khiar from a light snack into a main meal, tilit is how you do it. You can use plain torn bread, but fried bread is even better. If you prefer a thinner soup, replace the yogurt with buttermilk.

Even though it's not a heavy soup, abdoogh khiar is known for making people drowsy and helping them towards an afternoon nap. It's the perfect dish to have before siesta—we call it "chort zadan"—which is still a tradition for many people in Iran. At my restaurant, I would serve lunch, then close the doors at 3:30 pm, go home for a sleep, and return about 5:30 pm.

PREP TIME: 20 MINS **SERVES: 6–8**

1 lb 2 oz (500 g) Persian cucumbers, diced
2 green apples, cored and diced
1 cup (20 g) mint leaves, finely chopped
1⅓ cups (50 g) basil leaves, finely chopped
1 cup (50 g) dill fronds, finely chopped
1 cup (100 g) walnuts, crushed, plus extra
   chopped, to serve
1 packed cup (170 g) raisins
2 teaspoons salt
2 teaspoons freshly ground black pepper
4½ cups (1 kg) plain yogurt
6–8 ice cubes
4 teaspoons dried mint
Handful edible dried rose petals
Tilit (page 57), to serve (optional)

Combine the cucumbers, apples, herbs, crushed walnuts, and raisins in a large bowl, then stir in the salt and pepper. Add the yogurt and stir to combine, then add the ice cubes.

Divide the soup among bowls and top with the dried mint, chopped walnuts, and rose petals. Serve with tilit, if desired.

Ash Reshteh

NOODLE SOUP

This is the absolute number-one Iranian soup and one of the most important dishes in Persian cuisine overall. If soup was a royal family, this would be the king. "Ash" is a category of thick soups that are sturdy enough to be one-pot meals and "reshteh" (thread) is the name for the flat wheat noodles that help thicken this soup.

People eat ash reshteh when they have a cold or flu because it's so sustaining. It's also traditional to have it for Nowruz (Persian New Year), which happens towards the end of March, and it's one of the most popular dishes to give as nazri, a food offering that people give and receive as a blessing.

Kashk—a fermented dairy product—is also a distinctive ingredient in this soup. You can find it in Middle Eastern supermarkets in liquid or powdered form. As always, soak dried beans and legumes if you are organized but it's fine to use canned versions if you're not working ahead.

PREP TIME: 25 MINS + OVERNIGHT SOAKING IF USING DRIED BEANS AND LEGUMES
COOK TIME: 1 HOUR, 20 MINS **SERVES: 6**

½ cup (100 g) dried red kidney beans or
   1 x 14 oz (400 g) can, drained and rinsed
½ cup (95 g) dried chickpeas (garbanzo beans) or
   1 x 14 oz (400 g) can, drained and rinsed
½ cup (100 g) dried brown lentils or 1 x 14 oz
   (400 g) can, drained and rinsed
1 cup (250 ml) olive oil
2 yellow onions, 1 diced, 1 thinly sliced
5 garlic cloves, crushed
2 teaspoons ground turmeric
2 cups (60 g) cilantro, stalks and
   leaves finely chopped
2 cups (40 g) flat-leaf parsley, stalks and leaves
   finely chopped
9 oz (250 g) garlic chives, finely chopped
7 oz (200 g) spinach leaves
9 oz (250 g) reshteh ash (thick Persian
   wheat noodles)
2 teaspoons salt
2 teaspoons freshly ground black pepper
½ cup (15 g) dried mint
7 oz (200 g) liquid kashk (or plain yogurt), plus
extra to serve

If using dried beans and legumes, separately soak the kidney beans, chickpeas, and lentils in cold water overnight. The next day, drain, then transfer to three saucepans and cover with cold water. Cook the kidney beans and chickpeas over medium heat for 30–40 minutes, until soft, and cook the lentils over medium heat for 20–30 minutes, until soft.

Meanwhile, heat ½ cup (125 ml) of the olive oil in a large pot over high heat. Add the diced onion and cook for about 2 minutes until golden, then add half the garlic and half the turmeric and stir until fragrant. Add 8 cups (2 liters) water to the pot, along with the chopped herbs and spinach, and bring to a boil, then reduce the heat to a simmer and cook for 15 minutes.

Drain the kidney beans, chickpeas, and lentils and add to the pot along with the noodles. Simmer the soup for 15 minutes or until the noodles are cooked through. Season with the salt and pepper, then remove from the heat.

Heat the remaining oil in a large frying pan over high heat. Add the sliced onion and cook for 5 minutes until deep golden brown. Stir in the remaining turmeric until fragrant, then transfer to a bowl.

Add the remaining garlic to the pan and cook for 2 minutes until golden, then transfer to a bowl. Add the dried mint to the pan and cook, stirring, for 1 minute.

Divide the soup among bowls and swirl the kashk into the soup. Top with the fried onion, garlic, and mint and serve with extra kashk on the side.

Ash Doogh

YOGURT AND HERB SOUP

This yogurt soup holds very special memories for me. I grew up in Tehran but we often traveled to the Caspian Sea on the other side of Mount Damavand, the highest mountain in the Middle East. There are different roads that take you there but the most beautiful is Chalus Road, named after the coastal town that it leads to. About halfway between Tehran and Chalus, the famous Kandovan Tunnel burrows beneath the mountain range. On the southern side, the land is dry and brown but when you pop out of the tunnel after a five-minute drive, everything is humid and green. The world is transformed!

Once through the tunnel, street-food restaurants line the side of the road and all they sell is different kinds of ash (soup). Everyone stops. I always remember it: the drive, the tunnel, the change in weather and terrain, and the ash doogh that I loved to eat while looking out at the great view.

Doogh is a salty–sour yogurt drink; ash doogh is this drink turned into a thick soup, with lentils, chickpeas, and herbs. One spoonful and I'm back there, my face turned to the mountains.

PREP TIME: 20 MINS + OVERNIGHT SOAKING IF USING DRIED CHICKPEAS AND LENTILS
COOK TIME: 1 HOUR **SERVES:** 6

½ cup (95 g) dried chickpeas or 1 x 14 oz (400 g) can, drained and rinsed
½ cup (100 g) dried brown lentils or 1 x 14 oz (400 g) can, drained and rinsed
½ cup (125 ml) olive oil
4 yellow onions, diced
4 garlic cloves, finely chopped
2 cups (40 g) mint leaves, finely chopped
2 cups (60 g) cilantro, stalks and leaves finely chopped
2 cups (40 g) flat-leaf parsley, stalks and leaves finely chopped
9 oz (250 g) garlic chives, finely chopped
3½ oz (100 g) spinach, finely chopped
½ cup (100 g) jasmine rice
2¼ cups (500 g) plain yogurt
4 teaspoons all-purpose flour
2 teaspoons salt
2 teaspoons freshly ground black pepper

If using dried chickpeas and lentils, separately soak them in cold water overnight. The next day, drain the chickpeas and lentils, then transfer to separate saucepans and cover with cold water. Cook the chickpeas over medium heat for 30–40 minutes, until soft, and cook the lentils over medium heat for 20–30 minutes, until soft.

Meanwhile, heat the olive oil in a large pot over high heat. Add the onion and cook for about 2 minutes until golden. Add the garlic and cook for 1 minute or until fragrant, then add 8 cups (2 liters) water and the herbs and spinach. Bring to a boil, then reduce the heat to a simmer and cook for 15 minutes.

Drain the chickpeas and lentils and add them to the pot, along with the rice, and cook for 15 minutes. Reduce the heat to low and slowly add the yogurt, about a tablespoon at a time, stirring to combine, then gradually add the flour, stirring as you go. Cook the soup, stirring, for a final 10 minutes. Season with the salt and pepper, then remove from the heat.

Divide the ash doogh among bowls and serve.

Adasi

LENTIL SOUP

This is a thick lentil soup that's similar to Indian dal. We usually eat it for breakfast but sometimes later in the day, too. My mother would give it to me some mornings, telling me it would keep my brain working during the long day at school.

I love the bright kick of lemon juice, which is added at the end; some people make it with tamarind instead, getting the sourness that way. Iran's special golpar spice (Persian hogweed) works so well with sour flavors, so do seek it out in Middle Eastern supermarkets if you can.

PREP TIME: 10 MINS + 2 HOURS SOAKING TIME **COOK TIME:** 30 MINS **SERVES:** 4

3 cups (645 g) dried green lentils
½ cup (125 ml) olive oil
2 large yellow onions, diced
1 large potato, peeled and diced
1 garlic clove, finely chopped
Heaped 1 tablespoon tomato paste
2 teaspoons ground turmeric
1 teaspoon ground cumin
1 teaspoon golpar (Persian hogweed; optional)
2 large tomatoes, diced
8½ cups (2 liters) boiling water
2 teaspoons salt
2 teaspoons freshly ground black pepper
½ cup (125 ml) freshly squeezed lemon juice
Finely chopped flat-leaf parsley, to serve

Soak the lentils in a large bowl of cold water for at least 2 hours. Drain.

Heat the oil in a large pot over high heat. Add the onion and potato and sauté for 5 minutes or until golden. Add the garlic and cook for 1 minute, then add the tomato paste and cook, stirring, for another minute. Add the turmeric, cumin, and golpar (if using) and cook, stirring, for 1 minute until fragrant. Add the tomato and stir to combine, then add the drained lentils and cook for another minute. Pour in the boiling water, bring to a boil, then reduce the heat to a simmer and cook, stirring occasionally, for 20–30 minutes, until the lentils are cooked through. Season with the salt and pepper and stir in the lemon juice.

Divide the soup among bowls, top with a little parsley, and serve.

Ash Shole Ghalamkar

HEARTY BEAN, LAMB, AND RICE SOUP

This thick soup is my most favorite. The part of Tehran where I grew up is called Pasdaran and, like every neighborhood, there is a mosque. On the religious commemoration of Arba'een, our mosque would cook this soup for around 1,000 people. I was never very interested in religion but I really loved this day—I think because it was all about food.

For three days, people would prepare the ash (soup) and on the day of Arba'een, people would bring their big pots from home and we would fill them with soup. When I was a little kid, I loved watching the preparation, and from the time I was 14 I started helping. We would wash herbs, chop onions, make a fire, kill lambs, butcher them, and make the soup in 200 liter (53 gallon) pots. It was really exciting, with incredible energy and teamwork; a happy time, building to the community gathering on the final day. I wish I could go back to Iran to experience that again.

This is the recipe I learned in those days, though of course I've scaled it back quite a lot and you'll be relieved to hear that you don't need to kill your own lamb.

PREP TIME: 20 MINS + OVERNIGHT SOAKING IF USING DRIED BEANS AND LEGUMES
COOK TIME: 3 HOURS SERVES: 4–6

½ cup (100 g) dried red kidney beans or
   1 x 14 oz (400 g) can, drained and rinsed
½ cup (95 g) dried chickpeas or 1 x
   14 oz (400 g) can, drained and rinsed
1 cup (215 g) dried brown lentils or 2 x 14 oz
   (400 g) cans, drained and rinsed
⅔ cup (170 ml) olive oil
5 yellow onions, sliced
2 garlic cloves, diced
2 teaspoons ground turmeric
9 oz (250 g) boneless lamb shoulder or beef stewing
   steak, cut into ¼ inch (5 mm) thick slices
½ cup (100 g) jasmine rice
½ cup (100 g) barley
3½ oz (100 g) spinach, finely chopped
2 cups (60 g) cilantro, stalks and
   leaves finely chopped
2 cups (40 g) flat-leaf parsley, stalks and leaves
   finely chopped
3½ oz (100 g) garlic chives, finely chopped
2 teaspoons salt
2 teaspoons freshly ground black pepper
⅓ cup (10 g) dried mint
Liquid kashk (or plain yogurt), to serve

If using dried beans and legumes, separately soak the kidney beans, chickpeas, and lentils in cold water overnight. The next day, drain, then transfer to three saucepans and cover with cold water. Cook the kidney beans and chickpeas over medium heat for 30–40 minutes, until soft, and cook the lentils over medium heat for 20–30 minutes, until soft. Drain and set aside.

Meanwhile, heat ½ cup (125 ml) of the olive oil in a large pot over high heat. Add three-quarters of the onion and cook for 5 minutes until golden, then add the garlic and turmeric and stir for 1 minute or until fragrant. Add the lamb and 12 cups (3 liters) water, bring to a boil, then reduce the heat and simmer, covered, for 1 hour.

Using a slotted spoon, remove the meat from the pot, then shred using two forks. Return to the pot, add the kidney beans and chickpeas, and cook for 40 minutes. Add the lentils, rice, barley, spinach, and herbs and cook, stirring occasionally, for another 40 minutes, until the rice and barley are cooked through and the soup has a porridge consistency. Season with the salt and pepper.

Heat half of the remaining oil in a frying pan over medium–high heat, add the remaining onion, and cook for 4–5 minutes, until golden. Transfer to a plate, then add the remaining oil and the dried mint to the pan and fry for 30 seconds.

To serve, divide the soup among bowls and spoon over a little kashk, the fried onion, and fried mint.

Kaleh Joosh

POTATO, LAMB, AND SPLIT PEA SOUP

This hearty meat and yogurt soup always makes me smile, not only because of the taste but also because of the family story behind it. When my mother was pregnant with me, she went to a traditional hammam (bathhouse) with my four-year-old brother Hadi. All that time in the water made her very hungry, and when they arrived back home for lunch my grandmother had made kaleh joosh. My mother enjoyed it so much. She said she wouldn't trade it for anything in the world. She always told me that story with laughter and tears, and it's one that fills my heart. This is my grandmother's recipe.

PREP TIME: 30 MINS + 3 HOURS SOAKING TIME **COOK TIME:** 2½ HOURS **SERVES:** 8

½ cup (110 g) yellow split peas
½ cup (125 ml) olive oil
1 yellow onion, diced
2 teaspoons ground turmeric
1 lb 2 oz (500 g) bone-in lamb shoulder
8½ cups (2 liters) boiling water
2 teaspoons freshly ground black pepper
12 baby potatoes
¾ cup (50 g) finely chopped flat-leaf parsley, garlic chives, and cilantro
¼ cup (15 g) finely chopped spinach
1 tablespoon salt
4½ cups (1 kg) plain yogurt
8 garlic cloves, diced
½ cup (15 g) dried mint
Tilit (page 57), to serve (optional)

Soak the split peas in a large bowl of cold water for at least 3 hours. Drain.

Heat the olive oil in a large pot over high heat. Add the onion and cook for about 2 minutes, until golden. Add the turmeric and cook, stirring, for 1 minute until fragrant, then add the lamb and cook for 15–20 minutes, until browned on all sides. Pour in the boiling water and add the black pepper, then cover with a lid, reduce the heat to low, and cook for 1½ hours.

Add the drained split peas, potatoes, herbs, and spinach and cook for 30 minutes, until the potatoes are cooked through and easily pierced with a knife. Remove the pot from the heat and stir in the salt, yogurt, and garlic until well combined. Return the pot to high heat and bring to a boil, stirring frequently, then reduce the heat to low, add the dried mint, and cook for a final 10–15 minutes, adding a little more water if the soup is very thick.

Divide the soup among bowls and serve with tilit, if desired.

Hamed's Favorites

See over page for dishes

Hamed's Favorites

*If someone ever offered to make
a banquet for me, these are the dishes
I'd request. They are the recipes
that are most personal for me,
evoking the sweetest memories.
Luckily, they go well together, too!*

NOON LAVASH
Persian flatbread
57

KHORESH ALOO ESFENAJ
slow-cooked lamb with spinach
126

This is the most important chapter in my cookbook. These dishes are mostly traditional and often very significant in our culture. Some are more commonly found in restaurants, many are homey, others are reserved for special occasions. All of them have stories, whether historical or anchored in my own childhood. They all have meaning and I'm glad to share them with you.

When we say meat in Iran, we usually mean lamb, which is the most prized meat. Beef is cheaper than lamb and many dishes can be successfully made with either meat. Chicken is an everyday protein, cheaper than lamb or beef, yet often used in dishes that are lavish in flavor and presentation. Pork is not eaten in Iran because of Islamic prohibitions.

Mains

Fesenjun

WALNUT AND POMEGRANATE CHICKEN STEW

Two of the most well-known Persian dishes outside of Iran are ash reshteh (page 102) and fesenjun. This nutty, sweet and sour chicken stew is thickened generously with walnuts and pomegranate molasses, and given a romantic glow from saffron and turmeric. It's an incredible combination of flavors: expressive and seductive and so satisfyingly tasty.

Fesenjun's lavishness suggests it originated in the royal kitchens of the Persian Empire, and even today fesenjun is a labor-intensive and expensive meal for most people, so it's usually only made in restaurants and for special occasions, such as weddings.

My version is a simplified interpretation of this dish, but it's just as delicious. You can make it with duck instead of chicken and I've also added a vegan version on page 164. Walnuts are such an important part of this dish so they must be of the highest quality. They shouldn't taste rancid or bitter at all.

PREP TIME: 20 MINS COOK TIME: 40 MINS SERVES: 6–8

4 cups (400 g) walnut halves
½ cup (125 ml) olive oil
2 yellow onions, finely diced
2 teaspoons ground turmeric
2 teaspoons freshly ground black pepper
3 lb 5 oz (1.5 kg) skinless boneless chicken thighs
2 teaspoons salt
1 teaspoon ground nutmeg
Boiling water
1 cup (250 ml) pomegranate molasses
1 x quantity Saffron Liquid (page 214)
4 teaspoons sugar

TO SERVE
Pomegranate arils
Chopped flat-leaf parsley
Zereshk Polow (page 172)

Blend the walnuts and 1 cup (250 ml) water in a food processor for 3–5 minutes, until a paste forms.

Heat the olive oil in a large pot over high heat. Add the onion and cook for about 2 minutes, until golden brown. Add the turmeric and black pepper and fry for another minute, then add the chicken and brown for 2 minutes. Add the salt and nutmeg and enough boiling water to just cover the chicken. Reduce the heat to low, cover with a lid, and simmer for 25 minutes or until the chicken is cooked through.

Add the walnut paste to the pot, increase the heat to medium, and cook, stirring frequently, for 10 minutes, taking care not to burn the walnuts on the base of the pot. Add the pomegranate molasses and cook, stirring, for 5 minutes. Add the saffron liquid and sugar and stir until well combined.

Transfer the fesenjun to a serving dish and scatter pomegranate arils and parsley over the top. Serve with zereshk polow.

Baghali Polow Ba Mahiche

FAVA BEAN PILAF WITH LAMB SHANKS

Just about every restaurant in Iran serves this special two-part dish of lamb shanks and rice. It's quite a project so people don't often cook it at home, though I was lucky that my mother would sometimes make it as a special treat. I don't serve it on an everyday basis in my restaurant, but when I include it on catering menus the feedback is always overwhelmingly positive.

The name baghali polow ba mahiche translates as "fava bean" (baghali) "pilaf" (polow) "shank" (mahiche), and that pretty much describes the main elements, but without giving a sense of the majesty of this dish. The lamb is slow-cooked until it's very tender and the spice flavors become very deep and layered. The rice is studded with bright-green fava (broad) beans and—ideally—you'll take the time to make a crispy tahdig on the base of the rice. When it's inverted to serve, the crunchy, golden tahdig is the prized part of the meal.

Fava beans are only in season for a short time. When they're not available, use frozen fava beans instead.

PREP TIME: 15 MINS + 1 HOUR SOAKING TIME **COOK TIME:** 2 HOURS **SERVES:** 4

4 lamb shanks
2 yellow onions, halved
2 teaspoons ground turmeric
1 teaspoon ground cardamom
2 cinnamon sticks
Salt and freshly ground black pepper
Pomegranate arils, to serve
Chopped flat-leaf parsley, to serve

BAGHALI POLOW
2 cups (400 g) long-grain basmati rice
2 teaspoons salt
1 lb 2 oz (500 g) podded fava (broad) beans
4 garlic cloves, finely chopped
½ bunch dill, finely chopped
½ bunch cilantro, stalks and leaves
    finely chopped
1 cup (250 ml) olive oil
1 Noon Lavash (page 57) or store-bought Persian
    or Lebanese flatbread
1 x quantity Saffron Liquid (page 214)

To make the baghali polow, place the rice in a large bowl of cold water. Stir in 1 teaspoon of the salt and set aside for 1 hour.

Meanwhile, place the lamb shanks, onion, turmeric, cardamom, and cinnamon sticks in a large stockpot, cover with water, and place over high heat. Bring to a boil, then reduce the heat to low and simmer for about 2 hours (add an extra 1 cup/250 ml water if the mixture starts to dry out), until the lamb is tender and falling apart. Season with salt and pepper.

While the lamb is cooking, bring a small saucepan of water to a boil. Add the fava beans and cook for 5 minutes, until tender. Drain and refresh under cold running water, then peel the beans to reveal their bright-green interior.

Bring a pot of water to a boil. Drain the rice and rinse well, then add to the boiling water. Return to a boil and cook the rice for about 10 minutes, until tender. Stir in the fava beans, garlic, herbs, and remaining salt, then drain if necessary.

Remove the lamb shanks from the sauce, then transfer the sauce to a blender, discarding the cinnamon sticks, and blend to a smooth gravy. Pour the gravy into a clean saucepan and simmer over medium–high heat to thicken slightly, if necessary.

Pour the olive oil into large nonstick sauté pan and gently lay the flatbread on top. Spoon the rice over the top of the flatbread, then place the pan over low heat and cook, covered, for 15 minutes. Transfer 2 cups (370 g) of the cooked rice to a bowl and stir in the saffron liquid to make saffron rice.

To serve, invert the rice and tahdig onto a serving plate and spoon the saffron rice over the top. Divide the lamb shanks and gravy among shallow bowls and top with pomegranate arils and chopped parsley. Serve with the polow on the side.

Tahchin

LAYERED RICE CAKE

I know I've said a few dishes in this book are my favorite ... and this is another one. It's hard to choose a favorite child! You can think of tahchin as a savory cake, layered with chicken, rice, and barberries. Most Persian rice dishes are all about the fluffy rice but this dish relies on mushy rice held together with yogurt and butter. The base of the rice is cooked so it forms a crisp tahdig, and it's fragrant with saffron.

Most restaurants in Iran will serve tahchin but it's also made at home. I learned to make it in a restaurant in Tehran where we made it on a huge tray, but I make it in a smaller pan at home because my kids love this dish. It's a little tricky to cook but the payoff is worth it and the more you make it, the easier it will be to flip it out in the perfect shape. A nonstick sauté pan is a huge help.

PREP TIME: 1 HOUR, 20 MINS + 1 HOUR SOAKING TIME
COOK TIME: 1 HOUR **SERVES:** 8

3 cups (600 g) basmati rice
1 tablespoon salt
1¼ cups (310 ml) olive oil
11 tablespoons (150 g) unsalted butter
2 yellow onions, finely diced
2 teaspoons ground turmeric
3 lb 5 oz (1.5 kg) skinless boneless chicken thighs
2 teaspoons freshly ground black pepper
2 cups (500 ml) boiling water
1 x quantity Saffron Liquid (page 214)
1 cup (260 g) Greek-style yogurt
2 cups (140 g) dried barberries, soaked
   in cold water
½ cup (70 g) shelled pistachios, roughly chopped

TOMATO-BARBERRY CHUTNEY
2 tomatoes
2½ tablespoons tomato paste

Place the rice in a large bowl of cold water. Stir through 1 teaspoon of the salt and set aside to soak for 1 hour.

Meanwhile, heat ½ cup (125 ml) of the olive oil and 3½ tablespoons (50 g) of the butter in a large pot over high heat. Add the onion and cook for about 2 minutes, until golden. Add the turmeric and cook for 1 minute, then add the chicken, 1 teaspoon of the remaining salt, and the pepper. Reduce the heat to medium and cook the chicken, turning frequently, for 15–20 minutes, until golden brown. Add the boiling water, then cover, reduce the heat to low, and cook for 10–15 minutes, until slightly reduced. Add two-thirds of the saffron liquid (leave the threads behind) and continue to cook, covered, until the liquid has evaporated. Remove the pot from the heat.

Meanwhile, bring a pot of water to a boil. Drain the soaked rice and add to the boiling water with the remaining salt. Cook over high heat for 15–20 minutes, until very soft. Drain the rice and transfer to a large bowl. Add the yogurt, 3½ tablespoons (50 g) of the remaining butter, and all of the remaining saffron liquid. Stir to combine. Drain the barberries.

Place ½ cup (125 ml) of the remaining oil and all of the remaining butter in a large nonstick sauté pan and swirl the oil up the side of the pan. Add one-third of the rice mixture, then, using a slotted spoon, lay the cooked chicken on top of the rice. Add another third of the rice mixture and one-third of the drained barberries. Finish with the remaining rice and smooth the top. Set the pan over low heat, then cover and cook for 20–30 minutes.

Meanwhile, to prepare the tomato–barberry chutney, bring a saucepan of water to a boil over high heat. Score a cross into the base of the tomatoes. Add the tomatoes to the boiling water and blanch for 1 minute, then drain and immediately plunge into a bowl of iced water. Peel the tomatoes and roughly chop.

Add the tomato paste to the pan, along with the cooked onion, and set over high heat. Add the chopped tomato and one-third of the remaining barberries and cook, stirring, for 10 minutes, until thickened. Remove from the heat and set aside.

Heat the remaining olive oil in a frying pan over high heat. Add the remaining barberries and the pistachios and cook for 1 minute.

To serve, carefully invert the rice cake onto a serving plate. Scatter the fried pistachios and barberries over the top, then cut into wedges and serve with the tomato–barberry chutney on the side.

Pictured on pages 122–123

Tahchin (page 120)

Zereshk Polow Ba Morgh

BARBERRY PILAF WITH CHICKEN

This is a simple dish that my mom taught me. I could eat it every single day and never get bored with it because the combination of flavors is so special. The sweetness and fragrance of the rice, the sourness of the barberries, and the simple nourishment of the vegetables all combine to make it heavenly.

The chicken (morgh) is always served with zereshk polow (page 172), a jeweled pilaf in the vegetarian mains chapter.

PREP TIME: 15 MINS **COOK TIME:** 40 MINS **SERVES:** 4

⅔ cup (170 ml) olive oil
2 yellow onions, diced
1 teaspoon ground turmeric
2 garlic cloves, finely chopped
½ green bell pepper, diced
2 lb 4 oz (1 kg) skinless boneless chicken thighs
Heaped 1 tablespoon tomato paste
4 cups (1 liter) boiling water
1 carrot, cut into large chunks
1 cinnamon stick
2 teaspoons salt
2 teaspoons freshly ground black pepper
1 x quantity Saffron Liquid (page 214)
Zereshk Polow (page 172), to serve
Torshi Bademjan (page 183), to serve (optional)

Heat ½ cup (125 ml) of the olive oil in a large pot over high heat. Add the onion and cook for about 2 minutes, until golden, then add the turmeric and stir for 10 seconds. Add the garlic and bell pepper and stir for another 10 seconds, then add the chicken and cook, stirring frequently, for 5 minutes or until browned. Stir in the tomato paste for 1 minute, then add the boiling water, carrot, cinnamon, salt, and pepper. Bring to a boil, then reduce the heat to low, cover, and cook for 30 minutes or until the chicken is cooked through. Stir in the saffron liquid, then remove from the heat.

Heat the remaining oil in a large frying pan over high heat. Using a slotted spoon, remove the chicken from the stew, add it to the frying pan, and cook, turning occasionally, for 10 minutes, until crispy.

Transfer the sauce to a blender (discarding the cinnamon stick) and blend until you have a smooth gravy.

Serve the chicken with the zereshk polow on the side and the gravy for pouring over. Enjoy with torshi bademjan, if desired.

Khoresh Aloo Esfenaj

SLOW-COOKED LAMB WITH SPINACH

In Iran, our grandmothers and aunties always talk about healthy dishes, the ones with extra goodness and healing properties. Even my father has lots of books with herbal remedies and he'll tell me which tea to drink and which dish to eat if I'm not feeling well.

This slow-cooked lamb and spinach dish is one of those honored healing dishes—it tastes delicious but it's also loved because of its supposed medicinal virtues. My mom would make it sometimes and I was always grateful because it takes a long time to cook. Sometimes I felt guilty that she spent so long standing over the stove, only for us to eat it all in 10 minutes. But it didn't stop me eating!

This recipe calls for Persian dried plums which are very sour, and different from prunes, which are quite sweet. Look for golden or yellow sour plums in your local Middle Eastern supermarket. Any sour dish makes me smile, though this recipe also comes with a warning: our plums usually come unpitted and lots of Iranians have lost a tooth eating this dish. Be careful!

PREP TIME: 20 MINS **COOK TIME:** 1½ HOURS **SERVES:** 6

½ cup (125 ml) olive oil
3 large yellow onions, diced
2 teaspoons ground turmeric
2 lb 4 oz (1 kg) boneless lamb shoulder, cut into
    1¼ inch (3 cm) cubes
8½ cups (2 liters) boiling water
2 teaspoons salt
2 teaspoons freshly ground black pepper
2 lb 4 oz (1 kg) spinach, stalks and
    leaves chopped
10½ oz (300 g) aloo bokhara (golden dried
    plums; you can also use umeboshi or
    dried apricots)
Scant ½ cup (100 ml) pomegranate molasses
1 x quantity Saffron Liquid (page 214)
Saffron Rice (page 214), to serve
Shirazi Salad (page 90), to serve

Heat the olive oil in a large pot over high heat. Add the onion and cook for about 2 minutes, until golden, then add the turmeric and cook for 1 minute. Add the lamb and cook, stirring, for about 2 minutes until browned, then add the boiling water and salt and pepper. Bring to a boil, then reduce the heat to low, cover, and cook for 50 minutes, stirring every 15 minutes.

Add the spinach and aloo bokhara to the pot and stir well to combine, then continue to cook, covered, for another 30 minutes. Finally, stir in the pomegranate molasses and saffron liquid.

Transfer the stew to a serving dish and serve with saffron rice and Shirazi salad on the side.

Khoresh Karafs

SLOW-COOKED LAMB AND CELERY STEW

In Persian cooking, "khoresh" is a stew-like dish, usually cooked gently for a long time, and generally very hearty and filling. "Karafs" is celery, so this is a celery stew with lamb. This is a very homey dish, something your mother would make for you when you return home from a journey. It's not something you'd see in a restaurant. Making celery the hero of a dish might surprise you, but this is actually a magical combination of ingredients, especially when slow-cooked.

I've made a couple of tweaks to the classic recipe, adding pomegranate molasses and sugar: I like the balance of sweet and sour. Rice is a compulsory accompaniment, be it steamed rice, barberry rice, saffron rice ... it doesn't matter, as long as rice is on the table!

PREP TIME: 20 MINS **COOK TIME:** 1 HOUR, 45 MINS **SERVES:** 6

1 cup (250 ml) olive oil
3 large yellow onions, diced
2 teaspoons ground turmeric
1 bunch flat-leaf parsley, stalks and leaves finely chopped
½ bunch mint, leaves picked and finely chopped
2 lb 4 oz (1 kg) boneless lamb shoulder, cut into 1¼ inch (3 cm) cubes
4 cups (1 liter) boiling water
2 teaspoons freshly ground black pepper
½ bunch celery, trimmed and cut into 1¼ inch (3 cm) chunks
½ cup (125 ml) pomegranate molasses
Juice of 1 lemon
½ cup (100 g) granulated sugar
2 teaspoons salt
1 x quantity Saffron Liquid (page 214)
Cooked rice of your choice, to serve
Shirazi Salad (page 90), to serve

Heat the olive oil in a large pot over high heat. Add the onion and cook for about 2 minutes, until golden, then add the turmeric and cook for 1 minute. Add the herbs and stir through for 2 minutes, then add the lamb and cook for about 1 minute until starting to brown. Pour in the boiling water followed by the pepper and bring to a boil. Reduce the heat to low, cover, and cook for 50 minutes, stirring every 15 minutes.

Add the celery to the pot and stir, then cook for a further 30 minutes (check on the celery from time to time as you don't want it to get soft).

Stir in the pomegranate molasses, lemon juice, sugar, salt, and saffron liquid, then remove the pot from the heat and transfer the stew to a serving dish.

Serve the stew with your choice of rice and Shirazi salad on the side.

Gheymeh Bademjan

SLOW-COOKED LAMB, SPLIT PEAS, AND EGGPLANT

Gheymeh is a type of stew with lamb or mutton, split peas, and (usually) potatoes, though this version of the comforting dish is topped with eggplant instead. It's a very common traditional dish that you will find in any Iranian restaurant.

Balancing the richness of the lamb and the starchiness of the split peas is Persian dried lime, a very important Iranian ingredient, which you can purchase from most Middle Eastern supermarkets. When we say "dried," we mean it! Persian dried limes are very hard, almost leathery. To release their flavor, you poke the lime with a fork to pierce holes and cook it with the other ingredients. Lemon or lime juice is a decent substitute.

This gheymeh should be served with Shirazi salad (page 90) and your choice of rice.

PREP TIME: 20 MINS + 1 HOUR SOAKING TIME **COOK TIME:** 1 HOUR, 45 MINS **SERVES:** 6

1 cup (220 g) yellow split peas
1 cup (250 ml) olive oil
3 large yellow onions, diced
2 teaspoons ground turmeric
2 lb 4 oz (1 kg) boneless lamb shoulder, cut into
    1¼ inch (3 cm) cubes
Heaped 1 tablespoon tomato paste
8½ cups (2 liters) boiling water
2 cinnamon sticks
2 teaspoons freshly ground black pepper
4 Persian dried limes (or use ½ cup/125 ml freshly
    squeezed lemon juice)
1 eggplant, cut lengthways into
    ½ inch (1 cm) thick slices
2 teaspoons salt
7 oz (200 g) small vine-ripened tomatoes
1 teaspoon rosewater
1 x quantity Saffron Liquid (page 214)
Cooked rice of your choice, to serve
Shirazi Salad (page 90), to serve

Soak the yellow split peas in a bowl of cold water for 1 hour. Drain.

Heat all but 2½ tablespoons of the olive oil in a large pot over high heat. Add the onion and cook for about 2 minutes, until golden, then add the turmeric and cook for 1 minute. Add the lamb and cook for about 1 minute until starting to brown, then stir in the tomato paste until well combined. Pour in the boiling water followed by the cinnamon sticks and black pepper, then, using a fork, poke a few holes into the dried limes, add them to the pot, and stir. Bring to a boil, then reduce the heat to low, cover, and cook for 1 hour, stirring every 15 minutes.

Add the drained yellow split peas to the pot and stir, then continue to cook, covered, for 30 minutes, stirring every 10 minutes, or until the yellow split peas are cooked through.

Meanwhile, place the eggplant in a bowl and scatter over 1 teaspoon of the salt, tossing to combine. Set aside for 10 minutes to help draw out excess moisture and any bitterness from the eggplant, then pat dry with paper towels.

Heat the remaining oil in a very large frying pan over medium heat. Add the eggplant and tomatoes and cook, turning the eggplant frequently, for 5–10 minutes, until the eggplant is dark golden and the tomatoes are starting to collapse. Remove the pan from the heat.

Stir the rosewater, saffron liquid, and remaining salt into the lamb and yellow split peas, then remove from the heat and transfer to a serving dish (remove the dried limes and cinnamon sticks if you like). Spoon the eggplant and tomato mixture over the top, then serve with your choice of rice and Shirazi salad.

Ghormeh Sabzi

SLOW-COOKED LAMB AND HERB STEW

This thick slow-cooked lamb and herb stew is an essential Persian dish. Everybody in Iran loves it and our Afghan cousins are fans as well. Cooking large amounts of herbs like this might be foreign to most Western cooks, but it's a very typical Iranian technique. We love herbs fresh, we love herbs cooked, we just love herbs!

My mother cooked this dish a lot, and she'd make it in huge quantities. First we'd have the stew and later she'd give us a bowl of the hearty sauce by itself. I would be full but I'd always find more room for it! And then I'd wake up in the morning starving and have it for breakfast, too.

This is my mom's recipe. It's so delicious, but it's not quite the same as when Mom makes it. I'm not sure what it is. There's something about a mother's love that makes food taste even more amazing.

The trick to this dish is to chop the herbs finely and fry them well, until they reduce and almost melt, adding their soupy thickness to the lamb and beans.

PREP TIME: 20 MINS + OVERNIGHT SOAKING IF USING DRIED BEANS
COOK TIME: 1 HOUR, 45 MINS **SERVES:** 6

1 cup (200 g) dried red kidney beans, or
   2 x 14 oz (400 g) cans red kidney beans,
   drained and rinsed
1 cup (250 ml) olive oil
3 large yellow onions, diced
2 teaspoons ground turmeric
7 oz (200 g) cilantro, stalks and leaves
   finely chopped
7 oz (200 g) flat-leaf parsley, stalks and
   leaves finely chopped
7 oz (200 g) fresh fenugreek leaves, finely chopped
   (or use 1¾ oz/50 g dried fenugreek leaves)
7 oz (200 g) garlic chives, finely chopped
2 lb 4 oz (1 kg) boneless lamb shoulder, cut into
   1¼ inch (3 cm) cubes
8½ cups (2 liters) boiling water
2 teaspoons freshly ground black pepper
4 Persian dried limes (or use ½ cup/125 ml freshly
   squeezed lemon juice)
1 x quantity Saffron Liquid (page 214)
4 teaspoons rosewater
2 teaspoons salt
Saffron Rice (page 214), to serve
Shirazi Salad (page 90), to serve

If using dried red kidney beans, soak them in a bowl of cold water overnight. Drain and transfer to a large saucepan, cover with cold water, and place over high heat. Bring to a boil, then reduce the heat to a simmer and cook the beans for 30 minutes, until soft. Drain and set aside.

Meanwhile, heat the olive oil in a large pot over high heat. Add the onion and cook for about 2 minutes, until golden, then add the turmeric and cook for 1 minute. Add the herbs and cook, stirring frequently, for 10 minutes, until completely reduced. Add the lamb and cook for about 1 minute, until starting to brown, then pour in the boiling water followed by the black pepper. Using a fork, poke a few holes into the dried limes, then add them to the pot and stir. Bring to a boil, then reduce the heat to low, cover, and cook for 1 hour, stirring every 10 minutes.

Add the kidney beans and continue to cook for another 20 minutes, then stir in the saffron liquid, rosewater, and salt. Remove from the heat.

Transfer to a serving dish and serve with saffron rice and Shirazi salad on the side.

Sheet-Pan Saffron Salmon

There are lots of typical Iranian dishes in this chapter. This is not one of them! I invented this dish for my Australian friends and I love it, too. It's a Western idea but with Persian flavors, such as saffron and pomegranate molasses.

There's lots of lemon juice in this dish but you can adjust it to your own taste. I have to admit that I eat lemons like normal people eat oranges—you might not be quite as much of a lemon lover as I am.

Persian cooks would lean towards serving this dish with rice but you could just as easily cook it alongside a pan of potatoes. Fish and potatoes are a great combination.

PREP TIME: 10 MINS + 30 MINS MARINATING TIME **COOK TIME:** 40 MINS **SERVES:** 4

½ garlic bulb, cloves peeled
2 teaspoons salt
Zest and juice of 1½ lemons
4 x 8 oz (225 g) skin-on salmon fillets
1 x quantity Saffron Liquid (page 214)
2 teaspoons freshly ground black pepper
2½ tablespoons olive oil
¼ cup (65 g) tahini
¼ cup (60 ml) pomegranate molasses
Chopped flat-leaf parsley leaves, to serve
Ground sumac, to serve
Pomegranate arils, to serve

Place the garlic, salt, and lemon zest in a mortar and use the pestle to pound the ingredients to a paste.

Place the salmon in a dish and spread the garlic paste over the top. Combine half the lemon juice, the saffron liquid, black pepper, and olive oil in a small jug, then pour the mixture over the salmon. Set aside to marinate in the fridge for at least 30 minutes.

Preheat the oven to 350°F (180°C). Line a baking sheet with parchment paper.

Transfer the salmon to the prepared pan and bake in the oven for 15–20 minutes, until just cooked through.

Meanwhile, combine the remaining lemon juice, the tahini, and ⅓ cup (80 ml) warm water in a small bowl.

Place the salmon on a serving dish and drizzle with the lemony tahini and pomegranate molasses. Scatter parsley, sumac, and pomegranate arils over the salmon and serve.

TIP
If you'd like to serve this dish with roasted potatoes, toss some chopped potatoes in olive oil and roast in the oven for 40–45 minutes.

Persian New Year

See over page for dishes

Persian New Year

Nowruz, or Persian New Year, is one of the most important celebrations in Iran. These are some of the traditional dishes we prepare for the festivities.

KUKU SABZI
herb frittata
68

SABZI POLOW BA MAHI
fish with herb pilaf
140

KASHK E BADEMJAN
eggplant with kashk
64

TOMPOM SALAD
94

SIR TORSHI
pickled garlic
182

BAGHLAVA
baklava
192

CHAI E ZAFARAN
saffron tea
210

Sabzi Polow Ba Mahi

FISH WITH HERB PILAF

Sabzi Polow (page 169) is a very popular herbed rice dish and it goes brilliantly with this shallow-fried fish. When I think about serving fish with rice, I always remember my family sitting together eating and enjoying this dish.

It's up to you what kind of fish you use. I like to use salmon fillets, but small trout also work beautifully, as do sardines.

PREP TIME: 10 MINS + 30 MINS MARINATING TIME COOK TIME: 20 MINS SERVES: 4

½ garlic bulb, cloves peeled
2 teaspoons salt
4 x 8 oz (225 g) skin-on salmon or trout fillets
¼ cup (60 ml) freshly squeezed lemon juice
1 x quantity Saffron Liquid (page 214)
1 teaspoon ground turmeric
2 teaspoons freshly ground black pepper
1 cup (250 ml) olive oil
Chopped dill fronds, to serve
Sabzi Polow (page 169), to serve
Lemon wedges, to serve

Place the garlic and salt in a mortar and use the pestle to pound the ingredients to a paste.

Place the salmon or trout in a baking dish and spread the garlic paste over the top. Combine the lemon juice, saffron liquid, turmeric, and black pepper in a small jug, then pour the mixture over the salmon. Set aside to marinate in the fridge for at least 30 minutes.

Heat the olive oil in a large frying pan over medium heat. Add the salmon or trout, skin side down, and cook for 10 minutes, then turn the fish over and continue to cook for 5 minutes, or until just cooked through. Transfer the fish to paper towels to drain.

Place the salmon or trout on a serving dish and scatter the dill over the top. Serve with sabzi polow and lemon wedges for squeezing over.

Koofteh Tabrizi

STUFFED MEATBALLS

There are countless styles of koofteh (meatballs) in Persian cuisine. This dish is from Tabriz, my father's birthplace in northwest Iran, near the Azerbaijani border. It's not the easiest dish to make because every koofteh is stuffed with barberries and dried plums, like little treasures to discover as you eat.

Even though this dish is from my father's side of the family, the entire family on both sides agrees that my mother's koofteh tabrizi are the best. Her rendition was so beloved that she was often called upon to make it for big parties of up to 100 people.

PREP TIME: 30 MINS + 4 HOURS SOAKING TIME **COOK TIME:** 1½ HOURS **SERVES:** 4–6

2½ tablespoons olive oil
3 yellow onions, diced
2 teaspoons ground turmeric
⅓ cup (80 g) tomato paste
¼ cup (7 g) finely chopped flat-leaf parsley
¼ cup (12 g) finely chopped cilantro
8½ cups (2 liters) boiling water
2 teaspoons salt
2 teaspoons freshly ground black pepper
Tilit (page 57), to serve
Torshi Bademjan (page 183), to serve
Sabzi Khordan (page 214), to serve

KOOFTEH
½ cup (110 g) yellow split peas, soaked in cold water for 4 hours, drained
½ cup (100 g) long-grain basmati rice, soaked in cold water for 4 hours, drained
2 teaspoons salt
2 yellow onions, grated
1 lb 9 oz (700 g) ground beef
1 egg, lightly beaten
2½ tablespoons dried parsley
2½ tablespoons dried basil
2½ tablespoons dried tarragon
1 cup (70 g) dried barberries
Heaped 1 cup (125 g) coarsely chopped walnuts
4–6 aloo bokhara (golden dried plums; you can also use umeboshi or dried apricots)

Place the split peas and rice in separate saucepans, cover with cold water, and season the rice with the salt. Bring to a boil, then reduce the heat to a simmer and cook for 10–15 minutes, until soft and cooked through. Drain and set aside to cool.

Meanwhile, heat the olive oil in a large pot over high heat. Add the onion and cook for 5 minutes until golden brown, then stir in half the turmeric. Add the tomato paste and cook, stirring, for 1 minute, then add the herbs and stir. Pour in the boiling water, season with the salt and pepper, then reduce the heat to low, cover, and simmer while you make the koofteh.

Using a clean tea towel, squeeze out the excess liquid from the grated onion, then transfer to a large bowl and add the cooked rice and split peas, beef, egg, and dried herbs. Use your hands to bring the mixture together and knead for at least 10 minutes until you have a homogeneous meatball mixture.

Take a handful of the meatball mixture and roll it into a 2½ inch (6 cm) ball (about the size of a tennis ball). Using your finger, make a deep indentation in the ball and add 1 tablespoon each of the barberries and walnuts and 1 aloo bokhara. Enclose the filling with the meatball mixture and re-roll into a meatball shape, ensuring it is smooth with no cracks. Repeat with the remaining meatball mixture and filling ingredients to make 4–6 meatballs.

Remove the lid from the simmering sauce and increase the heat to medium. Bring the sauce to a boil, then gently lower the meatballs into the sauce and cook, partially covered, for 30 minutes. Roll the meatballs over and continue to cook for 20 minutes.

Transfer the meatballs and sauce to a serving dish and serve with tilit for dipping into the sauce and torshi bademjan and sabzi khordan on the side.

Ghalieh Mahi

FISH IN HERB SAUCE

It's fitting that I first ate this exciting fish dish in Bandar Abbas, a southern Iranian city on the Persian Gulf. This seaside town has a big fishing industry and busy seafood markets, which the families there make the most of.

"Mahi" means fish and "ghalieh" is the Arabic word for stew (what in Persian we call khoresh). In Bandar Abbas, the United Arab Emirates is just a stone's throw away across the Straits of Hormuz, and the Arabic language has been a big influence there.

The key elements of ghalieh mahi are fish, cilantro, and tamarind, creating a stew that's bright, sour, and bold. I like tuna, but you can use any firm-fleshed fish you like. Most people eat it with plain rice, but I recommend saffron rice.

PREP TIME: 20 MINS **COOK TIME:** 40 MINS **SERVES:** 4

½ cup (125 ml) olive oil
1 lb 2 oz (500 g) tuna steak, cut into
    1¼ inch (3 cm) cubes
2 yellow onions, diced
2 teaspoons ground turmeric
10 garlic cloves, finely chopped
7 oz (200 g) cilantro, stalks and leaves
    finely chopped
¾ cup (50 g) finely chopped fenugreek leaves
    or 1 oz (25 g) dried fenugreek leaves
2 tomatoes, grated
Generous ½ cup (100 g) tamarind paste
2 cups (500 ml) boiling water
2 teaspoons salt
2 teaspoons freshly ground black pepper
Saffron Rice (page 214), to serve
Lemon wedges, to serve

Heat 4 teaspoons of the olive oil in a large nonstick frying pan over high heat. Add the tuna and cook for 2 minutes on each side, until dark golden and cooked through. Remove the tuna from the pan and set aside.

Heat the remaining oil in the pan, then add the onion and cook for about 2 minutes, until golden. Stir in the turmeric, then add the garlic and cook for 1 minute or until fragrant. Add the cilantro and fenugreek leaves, reduce the heat to low, and cook, stirring, for 2 minutes, then return the tuna to the pan and cook for another 2 minutes. Add the tomato and allow to cook for 5 minutes.

Meanwhile, combine the tamarind paste and boiling water in a small bowl. Add the mixture to the pan, along with the salt and pepper, and cook, stirring occasionally, for about 20 minutes, until reduced and thick.

Serve with saffron rice and lemon wedges for squeezing over.

Tas Kabab

LAMB AND QUINCE STEW

This dish is named after a "tas," the huge copper pot it was traditionally cooked in years ago. It's an aromatic, gently simmered stew, which comes in different varieties all around our region, from Turkey to Albania.

The meat is sliced into long pieces rather than cubes and the vegetables are left very chunky so you can taste their individual qualities. We even add fruit: quince are great when they are in season and some people also add a squeeze of orange juice.

For a vegetarian version, replace the lamb with eggplant.

PREP TIME: 20 MINS **COOK TIME**: 1 HOUR, 10 MINS **SERVES**: 6

½ cup (125 ml) olive oil
2 yellow onions, diced
2 teaspoons ground turmeric
1 lb 2 oz (500 g) boneless lamb shoulder, cut into
    ½ inch (1 cm) thick slices
Heaped 1 tablespoon tomato paste
4 cups (1 liter) boiling water, plus extra if needed
2 quince, cut into large chunks (see Tip)
2 carrots, cut into large chunks
2 potatoes, peeled and cut into large chunks
2 cups (300 g) aloo bokhara (golden dried plums;
    you can also use umeboshi or dried apricots)
2 teaspoons salt
2 teaspoons freshly ground black pepper
Steamed rice, to serve

Heat the olive oil in a large pot over high heat. Add the onion and cook for about 2 minutes, until golden, then stir in the turmeric for 1 minute. Add the lamb and sear for 2 minutes, then stir in the tomato paste and cook for a further 1 minute. Pour in the boiling water and bring to a boil, then reduce the heat to low, cover, and simmer for 30 minutes, stirring occasionally.

Add the quince, carrot, potato, aloo bokhara, salt, and pepper to the pot and continue to cook, covered and stirring occasionally, for 30 minutes or until the quince and vegetables are soft and cooked through. If the liquid in the pot starts to dry out, add another 1 cup (250 ml) of boiling water.

Transfer the stew to a serving dish and serve with steamed rice.

TIP
Feel free to use firm pears if quince are not in season.

Kabab Torsh

SWEET AND SOUR KEBAB

You will find kebabs everywhere in Iran, but I particularly love this one from Gilan Province in the north, which lies between the Alborz mountain range and the Caspian Sea. Whenever we traveled to this region, eating this "sour kebab" was always part of the experience. And when travel wasn't on the horizon, my mother made her own version for us at home. The smoky charcoal flavor and aroma are so much part of the experience, so cook it on a charcoal grill if you can.

I suggest marinating the meat for at least 40 minutes, but longer—even overnight—is fine, too. Never use salt in marinades because it can toughen the meat. It's better to season your kebabs while they are cooking.

PREP TIME: 15 MINS + 40 MINS MARINATING TIME **COOK TIME**: 20 MINS **SERVES**: 4

½ cup (50 g) walnut halves
½ cup (125 ml) pomegranate molasses
1 large yellow onion, diced
3 tablespoons finely chopped mint leaves
3 tablespoons finely chopped flat-leaf
    parsley leaves
2 tablespoons finely chopped cilantro leaves
3 garlic cloves, roughly chopped
2 teaspoons freshly ground black pepper
2½ tablespoons olive oil
1 lb 2 oz (500 g) boneless lamb loin or beef chuck,
    cut into ¾–1¼ inch (2–3 cm) chunks
2 teaspoons salt
4 tomatoes, halved
4 long green chiles, halved lengthways

TO SERVE
Melted butter
Ground sumac
Noon Lavash (page 57) or store-bought Persian
    or Lebanese flatbreads
Sabzi Khordan (page 214)
Torshi Bademjan (page 183), to serve

Place the walnuts, pomegranate molasses, onion, herbs, garlic, pepper, and olive oil in the bowl of a food processor and process to combine.

Place the lamb or beef in a baking dish and add the marinade, making sure the meat is well coated. Set aside in the fridge for at least 40 minutes and up to overnight.

Light a charcoal grill and allow the coals to burn down to a coating of white ash.

Thread the lamb or beef onto metal skewers, then use the flat side of a large knife to repeatedly smash the meat on both sides to help tenderize it. Place the skewers on the charcoal grill and cook, turning frequently and seasoning with the salt, for 4 minutes on each side.

Meanwhile, alternately thread the tomato and chile onto metal skewers, then add to the grill and cook, turning occasionally, for 10 minutes, until blackened.

Transfer the lamb or beef skewers to a serving dish and drizzle melted butter over the top. Sprinkle with a little sumac and serve with the grilled tomato and chile, flatbreads, sabzi khordan, and torshi bademjan on the side.

TIP
You can also cook the marinated lamb or beef in a pot with 1 cup (250 ml) water. Cook over medium heat for 10 minutes.

Khoresh Bamieh

SLOW-COOKED BEEF AND OKRA

This khoresh (stew) is made with okra, one of my favorite vegetables. Most people in Iran make it with diced lamb or beef but I'd like to share my sister Mahnaz's version, using ground beef. This is just about the only dish that my mom takes second place in—my sister's version is the best!

A lot of people steer clear of okra because they think it's slimy. I actually love the texture but there are two ways to avoid it becoming gooey: first, keep the okra whole and, secondly, don't cook it for too long—30 minutes is plenty. If you're okra averse, maybe this will be the dish to turn you around!

PREP TIME: 20 MINS COOK TIME: 50 MINS SERVES: 4

4 tomatoes
2½ tablespoons olive oil
2 yellow onions, diced
2 teaspoons ground turmeric
1 lb 2 oz (500 g) ground beef
2 garlic cloves, finely chopped
2 teaspoons tomato paste
1 lb 9 oz (700 g) okra
2 teaspoons salt
2 teaspoons freshly ground black pepper
3 cups (750 ml) boiling water
½ cup (125 ml) verjuice or ½ cup (35 g) dried
  barberries
Chopped flat-leaf parsley leaves, to serve
Zereshk Polow (page 172), to serve
Sabzi Khordan (page 214), to serve

Score a cross in the base of each tomato. Bring a large pot of water to a boil over high heat. Add the tomatoes and blanch for 1 minute, then drain and immediately plunge into a bowl of iced water. Peel the tomatoes, then dice and set them aside.

Heat the olive oil in a large frying pan over high heat. Add the onion and cook for about 2 minutes, until golden, then stir in the turmeric and cook for 1 minute. Add the ground beef, garlic, and tomato paste and cook, breaking up the meat with the back of a wooden spoon, for 8–10 minutes.

Add the tomato and cook for 5–10 minutes, until reduced, then add the okra, salt, pepper, and boiling water. Bring the mixture to a boil and add the verjuice or barberries, then reduce the heat to low, cover, and cook for 20 minutes. Remove the lid and continue to cook for 10 minutes or until the mixture is reduced and thick.

Transfer to a serving dish and scatter the parsley over the top. Serve with zereshk polow and sabzi khordan on the side.

Jujeh Kabab

CHICKEN KEBAB

This is one of the most popular kebabs in Iran, enjoyed as street food and at family barbecues at home. I would say that every man in Iran knows how to make it. Jujeh means "baby chicken" but you can use any kind of poultry for this dish.

As with any skewered meat, it's best to cook it over charcoal to achieve that smoky flavor, but you can still experience the delicious marinade even if you end up baking the chicken in the oven.

An interesting feature of Persian kebabs is that we season them with butter once they're cooked. It's very distinctive and deeply delicious.

PREP TIME: 15 MINS + PLUS 4 HOURS MARINATING TIME **COOK TIME:** 30 MINS **SERVES:** 4

2 lb 4 oz (1 kg) skinless boneless chicken thighs, cut into 1½ inch (4 cm) cubes
2 yellow onions, chopped
1 green bell pepper, chopped
1 garlic clove, finely chopped
1 teaspoon lemon zest
1 cup (250 ml) freshly squeezed lemon juice
1 x quantity Saffron Liquid (page 214)
2 teaspoons freshly ground black pepper
1 teaspoon chile flakes
2 teaspoons salt
4 tomatoes, halved
4 long green chiles, halved lengthways
4 teaspoons olive oil

TO SERVE
Melted butter
Saffron Rice (page 214)

Combine the chicken, onion, bell pepper, garlic, lemon zest and juice, saffron liquid, pepper, and chile flakes in a large non-reactive bowl. Cover and set aside in the fridge to marinate for at least 4 hours, but preferably overnight.

Light a charcoal grill and allow the coals to burn down to a coating of white ash.

Remove the chicken from the marinade and thread onto metal skewers, then transfer to the grill. Cook the chicken, seasoning with the salt and turning the skewers occasionally, for 7–10 minutes or until cooked through.

Alternately thread the tomato and chile onto metal skewers, then add to the grill and cook, turning occasionally, for 10 minutes, until blackened.

Meanwhile, transfer the marinade to a blender and blend until smooth. Heat the olive oil in a saucepan over high heat, add the blended marinade ingredients, and cook, stirring occasionally, until reduced to a thickish sauce.

Transfer the chicken skewers to a serving plate and drizzle melted butter over the top. Serve with the grilled tomato and chile, reduced sauce, and saffron rice on the side.

TIP

To bake the chicken, preheat the oven to 400°F (200°C). Place the chicken skewers on a baking pan, transfer to the oven, and cook for 30–40 minutes, until cooked through.

Persian Makaroni with Tahdig

This is a culture-clash dish using spaghetti, which we—confusingly—call makaroni. I love Italian pasta dishes but I have to say we might have even improved on the original by adding a golden, crunchy potato tahdig to the recipe.

People mostly eat this dish at home. It wasn't something that my mom made but I had a friend called Mahyar and I would always ask him when his mother was making makaroni so I could come over and eat it! This dish brings back childhood memories, just not family memories.

A very thin angel-hair spaghetti is best for this dish. You can easily leave out the meat to make a vegetarian version.

PREP TIME: 20 MINS COOK TIME: 50 MINS SERVES: 4–6

1½ cups (375 ml) olive oil
4 yellow onions, diced
2 teaspoons ground turmeric
2 teaspoons freshly ground black pepper
10½ oz (300 g) ground beef
1 green bell pepper, diced
4 tablespoons tomato paste
2 tomatoes, diced
10½ oz (300 g) button mushrooms, sliced
2 teaspoons salt
1 lb 2 oz (500 g) angel-hair spaghetti
1 potato, cut into ¼ inch (5 mm) thick slices
Khiar Shoor (page 184), to serve

Heat ½ cup (125 ml) of the olive oil in a large frying pan over medium heat. Add the onion and cook for 10 minutes or until soft. Add the turmeric and pepper and stir to combine, then add the beef, bell pepper, tomato paste, and tomato and cook, stirring occasionally, for 10 minutes. Add the mushrooms and salt and cook for another 10 minutes or until the mixture is thick and reduced. Remove from the heat.

Meanwhile, bring a large pot of salted water to a boil. Cook the angel-hair spaghetti until al dente, then drain and mix the pasta through the sauce.

Heat the remaining oil in a large nonstick sauté pan over high heat. Add the potato and spread out the slices in an even layer to cover the base of the pan. Add the pasta and sauce, then cover with a lid wrapped in a clean tea towel, reduce the heat to low, and cook for 20 minutes.

To serve, carefully invert the pan onto a serving dish to reveal the potato tahdig. Alternatively, divide the pasta among plates and serve with the tahdig on the side.

Enjoy with khiar shoor.

Abgoosht

LAMB SHANK AND CHICKPEA HOTPOT

When I think about this dish, I start to feel sleepy. We used to eat abgoosht for weekend lunch when everyone in the family was home and my father was in charge of the cooking. It's a very heavy dish: we would eat it, have seconds, and then the whole family would take a "chort" (nap).

Traditionally, abgoosht is made in a stone pot known as a "dizi," and many dizi shops exist in Iran. Once the dish is ready, the pot is brought to the table to serve. The usual way to eat abgoosht is to start with the broth and tilit (soaked bread). After that, someone removes the lamb from the bones and mashes the meat and vegetables into a thick paste—"goosht koobideh," meaning "mashed meat." We would then eat that with bread. No wonder we needed a nap!

PREP TIME: 20 MINS + OVERNIGHT SOAKING IF USING DRIED CHICKPEAS
COOK TIME: 2 HOURS, 40 MINS **SERVES: 4**

½ cup (95 g) dried chickpeas or use 1 x 14 oz
   (400 g) can chickpeas, drained and rinsed
2½ tablespoons olive oil
2 bone-in lamb shanks, cut into three pieces
   (ask your butcher to do this for you)
2 teaspoons ground turmeric
2½ tablespoons tomato paste
12 cups (3 liters) boiling water
2 teaspoons freshly ground black pepper
4 baby potatoes
4 tomatoes, chopped
2 yellow onions, chopped into chunks
1 bird's eye chile, finely chopped
2 teaspoons salt

TO SERVE
Tilit (page 57)
Sabzi Khordan (page 214)
Torshi Bademjan (page 183)

If using dried chickpeas, soak them in a large bowl of cold water for 24 hours. Drain, then transfer to a pot and cover with cold water. Bring to a boil over high heat, then reduce the heat to a simmer and cook for 30–40 minutes, until soft and cooked through.

Heat the olive oil in a large pot over high heat. Add the lamb and turmeric and sear the shanks for 2 minutes, then add the tomato paste and cook, stirring to coat the lamb, for 1 minute. Pour in 8½ cups (2 liters) of the boiling water, followed by the pepper, and bring to a boil. Reduce the heat to low, cover, and cook for 1 hour.

Add the potatoes, tomato, onion, chile, salt, chickpeas, and remaining boiling water to the pot and continue to cook, covered, for a further 1 hour.

Remove the lid and check the water level—it should just cover the ingredients. If it's lower, then add more water; if there's still lots of liquid, increase the heat to high and cook until slightly reduced.

Remove the lamb shanks and, using two forks, shred the meat and return it to the pot. Discard the bones. Strain the broth into a serving bowl, then transfer the lamb and vegetables to a large serving dish and take both to the table.

To serve, invite guests to dip tilit into the broth for a first course, then invite someone to mash the lamb and vegetables into a thick mash. Serve the mashed stew with sabzi khordan and torshi bademjan.

Weekend Barbecue

See over page for dishes

Weekend Barbecue

*When you're firing up the grill,
why not do it Persian style?
I used to teach this combination of dishes
in a meat-focused cooking class and
everyone loved it.*

MAST BADEMJAN DIP
eggplant and yogurt dip
45

JUJEH KABAB
chicken kebab
153

ZEYTOON PARVARDEH
olive and walnut chunky dip

48

TORSHI BADEMJAN
eggplant pickle

183

KABAB TORSH
sweet and sour kebab

149

TOMPOM SALAD

94

AB HAVIJ BASTANI
Persian ice cream with carrot juice

212

Vegetables are the mainstay of Iranian cuisine. They're cheap, abundant, and easy to turn into accessible meals. Lots of people in Iran are poor so they naturally lean towards more frugal vegetable dishes, even if they would prefer to eat a bit more meat. But it means they are very creative, finding new ways to work with the same ingredients over and over again.

The dishes in this chapter are essential Persian vegetarian dishes, though I should also say that many meat dishes are easy to make meat free, often using eggplant or mushrooms.

Mains —
Vegetarian

Fesenjun Tofu

TOFU STEW

Fesenjun is one of the most loved dishes in Iran, and I didn't want vegans to miss out when I taught it in my cooking classes. My solution was to come up with this rich tofu and carrot stew. It has the soul of traditional fesenjun (page 116) but without the chicken, and the flavors are really beautiful. Some days I actually prefer this version to the original.

Make sure your walnuts are of the highest quality without any bitterness because they're a big part of the flavor and texture of this dish.

PREP TIME: 20 MINS **COOK TIME:** 40 MINS **SERVES:** 6

4 cups (400 g) walnut halves
½ cup (125 ml) olive oil
4 large carrots, cut into large cubes
1 lb 2 oz (500 g) firm tofu, cut into large cubes
2 teaspoons ground turmeric
2 teaspoons salt
2 teaspoons freshly ground black pepper
⅓ whole nutmeg, grated, or 1 teaspoon ground nutmeg
1 cup (250 ml) boiling water
1 cup (250 ml) pomegranate molasses
2 teaspoons sugar
1 x quantity Saffron Liquid (page 214)
Pomegranate arils, to serve
Finely chopped flat-leaf parsley leaves, to serve
Saffron Rice (page 214), to serve

Blend the walnuts and 1 cup (250 ml) water in a food processor for 10 minutes, until a paste forms.

Heat the olive oil in a large pot over high heat. Add the carrot and sauté for 5 minutes or until golden. Add the tofu and sauté for 5 minutes or until golden, then add the turmeric, salt, pepper, and nutmeg and cook for 1 minute or until fragrant. Add the boiling water and the walnut paste, then reduce the heat to low and cook, covered but stirring frequently, for 10 minutes. Stir in the pomegranate molasses and sugar and cook, stirring frequently, for 5 minutes, until slightly reduced. Remove from the heat. Stir the saffron liquid through the fesenjun.

Transfer the fesenjun to a serving dish and scatter pomegranate arils and parsley over the top. Serve with saffron rice on the side.

Yatimcheh

EGGPLANT AND POTATO HOTPOT

The name of this simple vegetable braise means "little orphan," which I think relates to the fact that eggplants and potatoes are the cheapest ingredients in Iran and the dish is a staple for very poor people. Perhaps because of the name, I wasn't a huge fan of this dish back home, but when I started making it in my cooking classes I developed a new appreciation for it. The gentle cooking and the subtle flavors make it a really satisfying dish and, of course, it's very nutritious.

You can easily increase the quantities and feed a crowd—my record is a banquet for 180 hungry people.

PREP TIME: 10 MINS **COOK TIME:** 40 MINS **SERVES:** 6

½ cup (125 ml) olive oil
2 large yellow onions, diced
4 garlic cloves, finely chopped
2 teaspoons ground turmeric
2 teaspoons salt
2 teaspoons freshly ground black pepper
2 large potatoes, scrubbed and cut into
    1¼ inch (3 cm) chunks
4 eggplants, cut into 1¼ inch (3 cm) chunks
2 carrots, cut into 1¼ inch (3 cm) chunks
4 large tomatoes, quartered
7 oz (200 g) button mushrooms (optional), halved
Finely chopped flat-leaf parsley leaves, to serve
Lemon wedges, to serve
Bread of your choice, to serve

Heat the olive oil in a large pot over high heat, add the onion, and sauté for about 2 minutes, until golden. Add the garlic and cook for 2 minutes until fragrant, then add the turmeric, salt, and pepper and stir to combine. Add the potatoes, eggplants, carrots, tomatoes, and mushrooms (if using) and pour in 2 cups (500 ml) water. Bring to a boil, then reduce the heat to low and cook for 30–40 minutes, until the vegetables are cooked through.

Scatter a little parsley over the yatimcheh and serve with lemon wedges for squeezing and bread on the side for mopping up the juices.

Adas Polow

LENTIL PILAF

This pilaf with lentils and caramelized onions (pictured over the page) is a great example of how adaptable Iranian dishes can be. The classic version includes ground beef, but when I started making it at the Asylum Seeker Resource Center in Melbourne, we didn't use meat so I had to be creative. I made it vegetarian, adjusted the flavor profile, and watched with happiness as this polow became a very well-loved dish.

This is such a comforting and satisfying polow, flavored with cinnamon, sweetened with golden raisins, and with the sturdy savoriness of rice and lentils. These honest staples are a good backdrop for the glamour ingredients: saffron, rosewater, and barberries.

I love to serve this with the Iranian eggplant pickle, torshi bademjan.

PREP TIME: 15 MINS + 1 HOUR SOAKING TIME **COOK TIME:** 30 MINS **SERVES:** 8–10

2 cups (400 g) long-grain basmati rice
2¼ cups (430 g) dried green lentils
1 packed cup (170 g) golden raisins
½ cup (35 g) dried barberries
⅔ cup (170 ml) olive oil
2 large yellow onions, diced
2 teaspoons ground turmeric
2 teaspoons ground cinnamon
2 teaspoons salt
1 teaspoon freshly ground black pepper
1 x quantity Saffron Liquid (page 214)
2 teaspoons rosewater
Torshi Bademjan (page 183), to serve

Separately soak the rice and lentils in cold well-salted water for 1 hour. Separately soak the raisins and barberries in cold water for 10 minutes and drain.

Drain the rice and lentils. Bring two saucepans of water to a boil. Add the rice to one pan and the lentils to the other. Bring to a boil again, then reduce the heat to a simmer. Cook the rice for about 10 minutes and the lentils for 15–20 minutes, until soft, but not overcooked and falling apart. Drain and combine the rice and lentils in a large bowl.

Meanwhile, heat ½ cup (125 ml) of the olive oil in a large frying pan over high heat. Add the onion and sauté for about 2 minutes until golden. Add the turmeric, cinnamon, salt, and pepper and stir until fragrant, then transfer the mixture to the bowl with the rice and lentils. Add the saffron liquid and rosewater to the bowl and stir well to combine.

Heat the remaining oil in the pan over medium heat, add the raisins, and cook for 1–2 minutes until heated through. Using a slotted spoon, transfer the raisins to paper towels to drain. Add the barberries to the pan and cook for 20 seconds, then also drain on paper towels.

Stir half the raisins and barberries through the polow, then transfer to a serving dish. Serve with the remaining raisins and barberries scattered over the top and the torshi bademjan on the side.

Sabzi Polow

HERB PILAF

When Persians think of rice dishes, it's not long before this herb pilaf (pictured over the page) comes to mind. It's a traditional New Year's dish, an essential accompaniment to fish (page 140), and also something people make when they feel like dressing up their rice.

As with so many rice dishes in Iran, we cook it twice: first boiling the rice until almost cooked, then recooking it in a pan with a bread tahdig at the base. Usually, we scoop out the rice, then remove the golden crunchy bread and cut it up to serve alongside. But you can also flip it over like a tahchin (page 120), so the beautiful bread is on top.

PREP TIME: 15 MINS + 2 HOURS SOAKING TIME COOK TIME: 30 MINS SERVES: 4

2 teaspoons salt
2 cups (400 g) long-grain basmati rice
1 bunch cilantro, stalks and leaves
     finely chopped
1 bunch dill, fronds finely chopped
4 garlic cloves, finely chopped
1 cup (250 ml) olive oil
1 Noon Lavash (page 57) or store-bought Persian
     or Lebanese flatbread
1 x quantity Saffron Liquid (page 214)

Fill a large bowl with cold water, add 1 teaspoon of the salt, and stir to dissolve. Add the rice and leave to soak for at least 2 hours. Drain.

Bring a large pot of water to a boil over high heat. Add the remaining salt, then add the rice and bring to a boil. Add the herbs and garlic and cook for 10–15 minutes, until the rice is just soft, but still has some bite (about 80 percent cooked). Drain.

Wipe the pot clean, add the olive oil, and place over low heat. Gently place the flatbread on top of the oil and spoon the rice mixture on top of the flatbread. Cover with a lid and cook for 15 minutes or until the bread is golden and crisp (you'll have to poke through the rice to check). Stir the saffron liquid through the rice, then remove from the heat.

To serve, spoon the rice onto plates, then break up the bread and serve it next to the rice. Alternatively, invert the rice and bread onto a serving plate, so the crisp, golden bread is on top.

Enjoy this rice dish with my fish recipe on page 140.

Sabzi Polow (left, page 169) and
Adas Polow (right, page 168)

Zereshk Polow

BARBERRY PILAF

Any special day must have this spectacular polow as part of the celebrations. It's guaranteed to provoke lots of excited exclamations when you put it on the table. The yellow rice, colored and fragranced by the saffron, along with the barberries and pistachios, make the dish look like a festival all by itself, and it is a wonderful accompaniment to fesenjun (page 116) or any kind of stew.

There's a special tahdig hidden at the base of the pot in this recipe. It's actually my brother Hadi's invention—he came up with the idea of adding a layer of crushed walnuts on top of the flatbread. It's really delicious.

PREP TIME: 15 MINS + 1 HOUR SOAKING TIME **COOK TIME: 35 MINS SERVES: 4**

2 teaspoons salt
2 cups (400 g) long-grain basmati rice
½ cup (35 g) dried barberries
1¼ cups (310 ml) olive oil
1 Noon Lavash (page 57) or store-bought Persian or Lebanese flatbread
½ cup (50 g) walnuts, roughly crushed
½ cup (70 g) shelled pistachios
4 teaspoons sugar
1 x quantity Saffron Liquid (page 214)

Fill a large bowl with cold water, add 1 teaspoon of the salt, and stir to dissolve. Add the rice and leave to soak for at least 1 hour, then drain. Soak the barberries in a bowl of water for 5 minutes, then drain.

Bring a large pot of water to a boil over high heat. Add the rice and remaining salt, return to a boil, and cook for 10–15 minutes, until the rice is just soft, but still has some bite (about 80 percent cooked). Drain.

Wipe the pot clean, add 1 cup (250 ml) of the oil, and place over low heat. Gently place the flatbread on top of the oil and scatter the crushed walnuts over the bread. Add the rice in an even layer, then cover with a lid and cook for 15 minutes or until the bread is golden and crisp (you'll have to poke through the rice to check). Remove from the heat.

Heat the remaining oil in a frying pan over high heat. Add the pistachios and cook for 10 seconds, then add the drained barberries and cook for about 30 seconds. Do not leave for longer than 1 minute, otherwise they will burn. Remove from the heat, add the sugar, and stir to combine.

Place the sweetened pistachios and barberries in a large bowl and add 2 cups (370 g) of the cooked rice. Stir in the saffron liquid until well combined and the rice is golden yellow.

Transfer the remaining rice to a serving plate and pile most of the saffron rice on top. Position the crispy bread on top of the saffron rice, then finish with the remaining saffron rice.

Lubia Polow

GREEN BEAN PILAF

This tomato and saffron rice with green beans isn't the most spectacular polow but it's actually my favorite. I grew up eating and making it with meat, but when I came to Australia I tried a vegan version and it's now my go-to way to make lubia (green bean) polow. It's comforting, healthy, and can easily be a meal in itself.

You can also make a tahdig following the method in the zereshk polow recipe (page 172).

PREP TIME: 20 MINS + 1 HOUR SOAKING TIME **COOK TIME:** 40 MINS **SERVES:** 4

2 teaspoons salt
2 cups (400 g) long-grain basmati rice
½ cup (125 ml) olive oil
2 yellow onions, diced
2 teaspoons ground turmeric
2 teaspoons freshly ground black pepper
1 lb 2 oz (500 g) green beans, trimmed and cut into
  ¾ inch (2 cm) lengths
4 tablespoons tomato paste
1 tomato, diced
1 x quantity Saffron Liquid (page 214)

Fill a large bowl with cold water, add 1 teaspoon of the salt, and stir to dissolve. Add the rice and leave to soak for at least 1 hour. Drain.

Bring a large pot of water to a boil over high heat. Add the rice and remaining salt, return to a boil, and cook for 10–15 minutes, until the rice is just soft, but not overcooked. Drain.

While the rice is cooking, heat the olive oil in a large frying pan over high heat. Add the onion and cook for about 2 minutes, until golden, then add the turmeric, pepper, and green beans. Cook, stirring frequently, for 5 minutes, then add the tomato paste and cook for another 5 minutes. Add the tomato and cook for a final 5 minutes, then remove from the heat.

Place 2 cups (370 g) of the cooked rice in a large bowl and add the saffron liquid, stirring to combine until the rice is golden yellow.

Gently mix the remaining rice with the green bean and tomato mixture. Add half of the saffron rice and stir to combine, then transfer to a serving plate. Top with the remaining saffron rice and serve.

Vegetarian Feast

See over page for dishes

Vegetarian Feast

It's easy to put together a vegetarian Persian menu. There are some dishes traditionally containing meat that I made vegetarian for the first time in Australia, so I could cater to more people in my cooking classes. I came to realize that they work very well and I often make them meat-free by preference now.

FELAFEL

56

MAST BADEMJAN DIP
eggplant and yogurt dip
45

NOON LAVASH
Persian flatbread
57

DOLMEH
stuffed vine leaves
55

YATIMCHEH
eggplant and potato hotpot
166

LUBIA POLOW
green bean pilaf
175

SHIRAZI SALAD
90

BAGHLAVA
baklava
192

Torshi (pickles) are a ubiquitous element in Persian culinary culture. We love the crunchy, sour contrast they bring to slow-cooked braises, thick soups, and fluffy rice dishes. We also love the way they preserve seasonal fruits and vegetables so we can enjoy them in different ways throughout the year.

And we appreciate their prettiness: there's something about the way sugar, salt, and vinegar react with fresh ingredients that makes them so appealing.

Iranian pickles are easily sourced from Persian food stores but it's fun to make your own, so I've shared some of my favorite recipes here.

Pickles &
Preserves

Sir Torshi

PICKLED GARLIC

Iranians are huge fans of sir (garlic). Fresh garlic is an essential component of many Iranian dishes, but we have a special place in our hearts for pickled garlic (pictured on page 187). Families have jars and jars of the stuff in the pantry and it's brought out for most meals. We eat it liberally with all kinds of dishes but especially polows (pilafs), seafood dishes, and our beloved herb omelet kuku sabzi (page 68). And when I say liberally, I mean it! When I was living at home, my father and brothers and I would each have a bulb of pickled garlic next to our plates and we'd eat a clove with every bite.

Sir torshi only gets better with age, becoming sweeter and milder the longer it pickles. Some people keep it for 20 or 25 years—I can't believe that a preserve can be as old as an adult!

PREP TIME: 10 MINS **PRESERVING TIME:** 1 YEAR **MAKES:** A HALF-GALLON (2 LITER) JAR

2 lb 4 oz (1 kg) whole garlic bulbs
1 cup (250 ml) white vinegar
1 cup (250 ml) apple cider vinegar
2½ tablespoons salt

Peel the first layer of papery skin from each garlic bulb, then wash the garlic and place the whole bulbs into a sterilized half-gallon (2 liter) glass jar (see Tips).

Combine the vinegars in a bowl and stir in the salt until dissolved. Pour the mixture into the jar, making sure the garlic is completely covered, leaving a ½ inch (1 cm) gap at the top. Cover with the lid.

Place the jar at the back of the fridge for a year, after which time the pickled garlic is ready to eat. When it's ready, open the jar and take out some garlic. Peel the cloves and enjoy them with your meal.

Store the pickled garlic in the fridge.

TIPS

To sterilize glass jars and lids, submerge them fully in boiling water for 10 minutes. Allow to air dry.

Traditionally, sir torshi is left to pickle for three years before being opened, but it keeps far longer and the garlic becomes softer as it ages. I once tried 15-year-old sir torshi. It was delicious—very soft and I could tell it was healthy—almost like an antibiotic.

My mother makes sir torshi every year and puts a date on the jar so she knows when she made it. She will then open the oldest jar of sir torshi in the pantry for us all to enjoy.

Torshi Bademjan

EGGPLANT PICKLE

Eggplant pickle (pictured on page 186) is probably my favorite Iranian pickle. Not only do I love the taste but eating it reminds me of making it with my mother when I was a child. Every summer, we would spend a whole day pickling 200 kg (440 lb) of eggplant, which was supposed to last the whole year but we'd usually finish it within three months! Everyone in my family—my three brothers, my sister, and me—loves pickles. Even though my mother would warn us not to open the jars for 40 days, we could never wait more than two weeks. She would be exasperated but I think she was also glad that we loved them so much. And I promise you, my mother's unripe pickles are fantastic. Make a double batch if you like these as much as I do.

PREP TIME: 50 MINS **COOK TIME:**15 MINS **PRESERVING TIME:** 2 WEEKS **MAKES:** 5 LB (2.25 KG)

1 teaspoon ground turmeric

2 cups (500 ml) white vinegar

½ cup (65 g) kosher salt

2 eggplants, cut into 1½ inch (4 cm) cubes

2 celery stalks, cut into ¾ inch (2 cm) cubes

1 carrot, cut into ¾ inch (2 cm) cubes

5½ oz (150 g) cauliflower florets, cut into ¾ inch (2 cm) cubes

½ garlic bulb, cloves halved

2 bird's eye chiles, halved

½ green bell pepper, cut into ¾ inch (2 cm) cubes

1 large tomato, cut into ¾ inch (2 cm) cubes

¼ bunch mint, leaves picked and finely chopped

¼ bunch cilantro, stalks and leaves finely chopped

¼ bunch flat-leaf parsley, stalks and leaves finely chopped

1 cup (25 g) tarragon, stalks and leaves finely chopped

2 teaspoons golpar (Persian hogweed)

2 teaspoons nigella seeds

Half-fill a large pot with water, then place over high heat and bring to a boil. Add the turmeric, ½ cup (125 ml) of the vinegar, half the salt, and the eggplant. Boil the eggplant for 10–15 minutes, until soft (but not falling apart), then drain and set aside to cool.

Place the cooled eggplant in a large bowl and add the remaining ingredients except the remaining vinegar and salt. Toss the ingredients together until the vegetables and herbs are well coated in the golpar and nigella seeds.

Divide the mixture among large sterilized glass jars (see Tip on opposite page), making sure that each jar has an even distribution of ingredients. Combine the remaining vinegar and salt in a large jug and stir in 1 cup (250 ml) cold water. Pour the pickling liquid over the vegetables, filling to the rim of each jar. Cover the jars with the lids, then give them a good shake. Open them up again to let the air out and add more pickling liquid to any jars that are no longer full.

Place the jars at the back of the fridge and leave them to pickle for 2 weeks, shaking the jars at the end of the first week.

Store the eggplant pickle in the fridge. Once opened, it will keep for up to 6 months.

You can serve the eggplant pickle with anything you like, but I particularly love to eat it with Koofteh Tabrizi (page 142), Abgoosht (page 156), and Adas Polow (page 168).

Khiar Shoor

PERSIAN PICKLED CUCUMBERS

Khiar (cucumber) shoor (salty) is what we call the cucumber pickles that are an essential part of Persian cuisine (pictured over the page). We add them to sandwiches and salads, such as olovieh (page 96), and they're ever present as snacks at the start of a meal. Their tart crunch also means they're an excellent side dish with kotlets (page 67), kuku sibzamini (page 70), and Persian makaroni (page 154).

My mother used to make these with firm, almost seedless, Persian cucumbers; if you can't find those you should look for pickling cucumbers.

PREP TIME:15 MINS **PRESERVING TIME:** 1–4 WEEKS **MAKES:** A HALF-GALLON (2 LITER) JAR

1 cup (250 ml) white vinegar
¼–½ cup (30–65 g) kosher salt (depending on how salty you like them)
2 cups (500 ml) boiling water (as needed)
2 lb 4 oz (1 kg) Persian or pickling cucumbers
3 bird's eye chiles, chopped
½ cup (30 g) chopped dill fronds
1 whole garlic bulb, cloves peeled
½ cup (15 g) chopped celery leaves

Combine the vinegar, salt, and boiling water in a large heatproof bowl, stirring to dissolve the salt. Set aside to cool to room temperature.

Tightly pack the cucumbers into a half-gallon (2 liter) sterilized glass jar (see Tip on page 182) with the remaining ingredients, and cover with the pickling liquid, filling to the rim of the jar. Seal with the lid and give the jar a shake, then open it up to release any air and top up with more pickling liquid if necessary.

Seal tightly and place at the back of the fridge for 1–4 weeks, shaking the jar every week. The longer you leave the cucumbers to pickle, the more flavorful they will be.

Once opened, store the pickled cucumbers in the fridge, where they will keep for up to 6 months.

Morabba Beh

QUINCE JAM

Quince is a beautiful, fragrant fruit but you can't eat it fresh—it's way too hard and very tart. We cook quince in tas kabab (page 146) and it's also nice turned into tea (page 211), but my favorite thing to do with quince is to make jam.

I always made this delicately spiced jam with my mother. It takes a while to cook but it's not difficult. Eating it is even easier! In Iran, we spoon thick cream onto flatbread, then dollop quince jam over the top and have it for breakfast. It's such a nice way to start the day.

This recipe makes enough to fill two jam jars but you can double the recipe if you have more fruit to use.

PREP TIME: 10 MINS **COOK TIME:** 1½ HOURS **MAKES:** ABOUT 2 JAM JARS

1 lb 12 oz (800 g) quince (about 2), seeds removed and cut into ½ inch (1 cm) cubes
2½ cups (500 g) granulated sugar
2½ tablespoons freshly squeezed lemon juice
6 cardamom pods, lightly crushed
4 teaspoons rosewater

Place the quince, sugar, lemon juice, cardamom, and 2 cups (450 ml) water in a large pot. Bring to a boil over high heat, then reduce the heat to low, cover, and cook gently for 1½ hours.

Lift the lid and check the color and consistency of the jam—it should be light red with a syrupy texture. To make sure the jam is set, place a tablespoon of the jam on a cold plate and run the end of a teaspoon through the jam. If the jam doesn't fill the space left by the spoon then it is set; if liquid pools into the space left behind, cook for a few more minutes and check again.

Stir in the rosewater and cook for 1 minute, then remove from the heat and allow to cool. Spoon the jam into sterilized jam jars (see Tip on page 182), then store in the refrigerator.

Once opened, the jam will keep in the fridge for up to 6 months.

From left to right: Torshi Bademjan (page 183),
Morabba Havij (page 188), Torshi Bademjan
(in jar), Morabba Albaloo (page 189), Sir Torshi
(page 182), Khiar Shoor (page 184)

Morabba Havij

CARROT JAM

Havij (carrot) morabba (jam) might sound strange, but I promise you it's delicious. It's a very traditional preserve in Iran and is always fed to soldiers doing their army service because carrots are so cheap. I have to admit I got sick of it during my two-year stint in the military but I'm back to enjoying it now, especially this version with saffron and cardamom (pictured on page 186). It's great spread on flatbread or toast with butter, and is lovely with feta, too.

Carrot doesn't set very firmly so you can add a little gelatine powder if you want. Otherwise, it will be a lovely drizzling consistency.

PREP TIME: 10 MINS **COOK TIME:** 1 HOUR **MAKES:** 2 LB 4 OZ (1 KG)

1 lb 2 oz (500 g) carrots, grated
1¼ cups (250 g) granulated sugar
5 cardamom pods, lightly crushed
2 teaspoons gelatine powder, bloomed in
   2 teaspoons cold water (if you
   prefer a firmer jam; optional)
4 teaspoons Saffron Liquid (page 214)
4 teaspoons rosewater
4 teaspoons freshly squeezed lemon juice
Pinch of salt

Place the carrots and 3 cups (750 ml) water in a large pot over high heat. Bring to a boil, then add the sugar, cardamom pods, and gelatine (if using). Reduce the heat to low, cover, and cook for 1 hour, adding more water if the mixture starts to look dry (see Tip).

Lift the lid and check the consistency of the jam—it should have a syrupy texture. To make sure the jam is set, place a tablespoon of the jam on a cold plate and run the end of a teaspoon through the jam. If the jam doesn't fill the space left by the spoon then it is set; if liquid pools into the space left behind, cook for a few more minutes and check again.

Add the saffron liquid, rosewater, lemon juice, and salt and stir to combine. Remove from the heat and set aside to cool to room temperature. Spoon the carrot jam into sterilized jam jars (see Tip on page 182) and store in the fridge.

Once opened, the jam will keep in the fridge for up to 3 months.

TIP
Jams always thicken upon cooling, so if your jam starts to dry out in the pot while cooking, don't be tempted to leave it or it will burn. Keep adding water to maintain a fairly runny consistency.

Morabba Albaloo

SOUR CHERRY JAM

Albaloo (sour cherries) are a highlight of the Iranian summer and my family would always make jam with them (pictured on page 186). My older brother Mehdi and I would visit a sour cherry farm and pick around 20 kg (44 lb) of fruit. When we made it home—hopefully not eating too many cherries on the way—we would help my mom make the jam. We'd also freeze some of the cherries to make sour cherry tea (page 211) in winter.

It's not always easy to find sour cherries but they are briefly available in mid-summer. You can also buy them frozen from Persian supermarkets.

PREP TIME: OVERNIGHT **COOK TIME:** 1 HOUR **MAKES:** ABOUT 4 JAM JARS

2 lb 4 oz (1 kg) pitted sour cherries
2½ cups (500 g) granulated sugar

Place the cherries and sugar in a pot and set aside to infuse overnight.

The next day, pour 3 cups (750 ml) water into the pot with the cherries and sugar and cook over very low heat for about 1 hour, skimming any foam that rises to the surface and adding a little more water if the mixture starts to look dry.

Lift the lid and check the consistency of the jam—it should have a syrupy texture. To make sure the jam is set, place a tablespoon of the jam on a cold plate and run the end of a teaspoon through the jam. If the jam doesn't fill the space left by the spoon then it is set; if liquid pools into the space left behind, boil for a few more minutes and check again.

Remove from the heat and set aside to cool to room temperature. Spoon the cherry jam into sterilized jam jars (see Tip on page 182) and store in the fridge.

Once opened, the jam will keep in the fridge for up to 6 months.

In Iran, we don't really eat dessert at the end of a meal but we do eat a lot of shirini (sweets). Every street has a shirini shop and every town has its own preferred variety of sweet treats.

We love sugary food any time of day. It's never the wrong time for a sugar rush! I don't ever remember having coffee without three sugars and although we will sometimes drink unsweetened tea, it's usually accompanied with shirini.

It would also be unthinkable to have guests arrive without having something sweet to offer them. As soon as we heard our aunties and uncles were visiting, my mother would either reach for the sugar jar or send one of us to the shirini shop for a box of something special.

Sweets

Baghlava

BAKLAVA

There are different types of baklava all around the Middle East and Aegean, though the Iranian version is more crisp and less sweet than Turkish or Greek baklava. I learned this recipe in Tehran, working at a pastry shop. There was an old man who made it and he didn't want to teach me so I had to sneakily watch him to learn the method!

It's a bit of a process to make, but it's not hard and the reward is great! I eat baghlava for breakfast, afternoon tea, evening tea, and before I go to bed—any time is the right time.

PREP TIME: 40 MINS **COOK TIME:** 20 MINS **MAKES:** ABOUT 30

1 cup and 2 tablespoons (250 g) unsalted butter, melted (use vegan butter for dairy-free baghlava)
Generous 4 cups (500 g) walnuts or shelled pistachios, plus extra crushed shelled pistachios for sprinkling
Twenty 18 x 14 inch (45 x 35 cm) sheets filo pastry (about 13 oz/375 g)
2½ tablespoons vegetable oil

BAGHLAVA SYRUP
½ cup (65 g) cardamom pods
1½ cups (300 g) organic or white granulated sugar
2½ tablespoons glucose syrup or honey
4 teaspoons freshly squeezed lemon juice
⅓ cup (80 ml) rosewater

Preheat the oven to 400°F (200°C). Grease an 18 by 13 inch (45 x 33 cm) baking sheet with a little of the melted butter.

Place the nuts in a food processor and process until crushed.

Lay one sheet of filo pastry in the baking sheet and brush the top with melted butter. Repeat the process until you have 5 layered sheets of pastry. Brush the top layer with butter, then sprinkle a layer of crushed nuts over the top. Separate out 5 sheets of the remaining filo pastry and reserve. Layer the remaining 10 filo sheets in the pan, brushing with butter and sprinkling with nuts between each layer, until all the sheets and nuts are used. Top with the 5 reserved sheets of filo, brushing with butter in between each layer. Leave the top plain.

Cut the baghlava in the pan in a diamond pattern, then brush with the vegetable oil, transfer to the oven, and bake for 20 minutes or until golden.

Meanwhile, to make the syrup, place 3 cups (750 ml) water in a pot, bring to a boil over high heat, then reduce the heat to low. Crush the cardamom pods using a mortar and pestle, then add to the pot and simmer for 10 minutes. Add the sugar and simmer for 5 minutes, then stir in the glucose syrup or honey and remove from the heat. Add the lemon juice and rosewater and stir to combine.

Allow the baghlava to cool for 5 minutes, then pour over the warm syrup and sprinkle with extra crushed pistachios. Allow the syrup to soak into the baghlava for 1 hour. Enjoy!

Persian Love Cake

Funnily enough, I only discovered Persian love cake when I came to Australia, but I think that since it's taken the world by storm it's also become more popular in Iran. For me, the key flavor combination is nutmeg and yogurt. There's something about it that is pure dessert alchemy.

Why "love cake"? The story goes that a village woman tried to woo a prince with this cake. He swooned over the cake but rejected the girl and she ended up eating it all herself. I hope your romantic cake adventures are more successful, though I have to say that eating the cake is also winning!

PREP TIME: 15 MINS **COOK TIME:** 40 MINS **SERVES:** 8–10

3½ cups (300 g) almond meal
1 cup (180 g) superfine or granulated sugar
1 cup lightly packed (185 g) light brown sugar
½ cup (125 g) unsalted butter, softened and
  cut into cubes
2 eggs
1 cup (260 g) Greek-style yogurt
1 teaspoon salt
2 teaspoons ground cardamom
2 teaspoons ground nutmeg
½ cup (50 g) sliced almonds
¼ cup (35 g) slivered pistachios
Edible dried rose petals, to serve (optional)

Preheat the oven to 300°F (150°C). Grease an 8 inch (20 cm) round cake pan.

Combine the almond meal, sugars, and butter in a large bowl and mix with your fingers until the mixture resembles breadcrumbs. Press half the crumb mixture into the cake pan, creating an even base.

Add the eggs, yogurt, salt, and spices to the remaining crumb mixture in the bowl, and, using a wooden spoon, mix until smooth. Pour the batter into the pan and smooth the surface with a spatula. Sprinkle the sliced almonds and pistachios on top.

Transfer to the oven and bake for 1 hour, until a skewer inserted into the center of the cake comes out clean. Start checking after the 50 minute mark to ensure it's not coloring too quickly and cover the cake with foil if necessary.

Allow the cake to cool in the pan for 10 minutes, then turn out onto a wire rack to cool completely. Decorate with dried rose petals (if using) and serve.

The cake will keep in an airtight container in the fridge for 3–4 days.

Bliss Balls

When I came to Australia and started enjoying the cafe culture I saw bliss balls and protein balls everywhere. I thought surely I can do a Persian version of these, as we already have the building blocks. One of our simple but famous snacks is walnut-stuffed dates. Tahini is a popular ingredient in sweet dishes, often swirled through grape molasses for a breakfast dip. Cardamom is a traditional spice for sweets, while vanilla adds a more modern touch.

These bliss balls are a multicultural mash-up in one exciting mouthful. They're one of the most popular sweets at my cafe—maybe they will be at your place as well.

PREP TIME: 15 MINS MAKES: 10

1 cup (100 g) walnut halves
7 oz (200 g) soft dates (preferably Persian), pitted
Generous ⅓ cup (100 g) tahini
2 teaspoons vanilla extract
1 teaspoon ground cardamom

SUGGESTED COATINGS
Generous 1 cup (130 g) slivered almonds
1 cup (130 g) slivered shelled pistachios
1 cup (150 g) sesame seeds
1 cup (15 g) edible dried rose petals
1 cup (65 g) dried barberries

Crush the walnuts using a mortar and pestle or in the bowl of a food processor. Transfer to a bowl.

Place the dates, half the tahini, the vanilla extract, and ground cardamom in the bowl of the food processor and process until well combined. Transfer to the bowl with the walnuts and mix well. Add the remaining tahini and, using your hands, mix to form a dough.

Roll the mixture into 10 even-sized balls, then roll in your chosen coating to finish—I like to use a mixture of slivered pistachios and barberries.

The bliss balls will keep in an airtight container in the fridge for 1–2 weeks

Khagineh

SUGAR PANCAKE

This is a quick and tasty dessert or breakfast that's common in the north and western parts of Iran. It's kind of like a syrup-topped pancake; my mother would cook it in the pan, cut it like a pizza, and serve it to us after we ate ash (soup), which was usually salty and sour so we'd always feel like something sweet afterwards.

I love this dish because of the beautiful fragrant flavors: saffron, cardamom, vanilla, cinnamon, and rose all combining to create a beautiful experience. It's an easy dessert to have in your repertoire.

PREP TIME: 5 MINS **COOK TIME:** 10 MINS **SERVES:** 4

½ cup (110 g) granulated sugar
½ teaspoon saffron threads
½ teaspoon ground cinnamon
½ teaspoon vanilla extract
½ teaspoon ground cardamom
3 eggs
4 teaspoons all-purpose flour
½ cup (130 g) plain yogurt
½ cup (60 g) crushed walnuts
2½ tablespoons unsalted butter or vegetable oil
Edible dried rose petals, to serve
Shelled pistachios, to serve

Place 1½ cups (375 ml) water, the sugar, and spices in a small saucepan and bring to a boil over medium heat.

Meanwhile, whisk together the eggs, flour, and yogurt in a large bowl, then stir in the crushed walnuts.

Heat the butter or oil in a large frying pan over low heat. Pour in the batter and cook the pancake for 2 minutes on each side. Increase the heat to high and pour in the hot syrup. Allow most of the syrup to soak into the pancake, then remove from the heat.

Transfer the pancake to a serving plate and scatter the rose petals and pistachios over the top. Cut into slices and serve.

Bastani Sonnati

PERSIAN ICE CREAM

You can make this traditional Persian ice cream from scratch but the easy way to do it is to buy vanilla ice cream and add the Persian ingredients. I do this in my cafe because I don't have an ice cream maker so you definitely have permission to do it at home!

My key memory of bastani sonnati is eating it with my father at a shop near the army base he worked at. During the long summer vacation, there was an activity camp there and I'd go three days a week for swimming classes, religious instruction, and soccer. When Dad picked me up at the end of the day, we'd always stop for ice cream on the way home. I loved that shop! And even when I grew up, I would travel from north Tehran to this particular one in the south of the city, probably passing 100 ice cream shops along the way, just because it was so good. See also ab havij bastani (page 212).

PREP TIME: 10 MINS + 6 HOURS FREEZING TIME **SERVES:** 8

1 cup (250 ml) heavy whipping cream
8 cups (2 liters) creamy vanilla ice cream
    (pistachio ice cream also works well)
1 cup (130 g) chopped shelled pistachios, plus extra
    to serve (optional)
2½ tablespoons Saffron Liquid (page 214)
2½ tablespoons rosewater
Edible dried rose petals, to serve

Pour the cream into an 8 x 12 inch (20 x 30 cm) baking dish, then set aside in the freezer for 2 hours.

Remove the frozen cream from the freezer and cut it into ¾ inch (2 cm) squares (it will shatter, so your squares won't be even, but this is fine). Return the cream blocks to the freezer.

Refrigerate the vanilla ice cream for 15–20 minutes to soften slightly, then add the pistachios, saffron liquid, rosewater, and cream blocks and stir until well combined. Return the ice cream to the freezer for 1–2 hours until firm.

Spoon the ice cream into bowls and top with rose petals and a few extra pistachios, if you like. Serve immediately. Enjoy!

Orumiyeh Saffron Halva

HALVA SLICES

*I was born in Orumiyeh, in Western Iran near the Turkish border, and even though
we moved to Tehran when I was one, I still have a fondness for the food of my birthplace.
This halva is my favorite sweet and whenever I went back to Orumiyeh I would always request
it and enjoy it with black tea. The traditional version is quite syrupy and you eat it with a spoon,
but this one is can be sliced.*

PREP TIME: 10 MINS **COOK TIME:** 20 MINS **SERVES:** 8

Pinch (1 g) saffron threads
2¼ cups (440 g) granulated sugar
14 tablespoons (200 g) unsalted butter
1¼ cups (150 g) all-purpose flour
4 teaspoons rosewater
1 teaspoon ground cardamom
1 cup (100 g) walnut halves
Generous 1 cup (140 g) shelled pistachios
Large handful edible dried rose petals, to serve

Place 3 cups (750 ml) water in a small saucepan and bring to a boil over high heat.

Meanwhile, using a mortar and pestle, grind the saffron threads and 4 teaspoons of the sugar to a powder.

Melt the butter in a pot over medium heat. Sift the flour into the melted butter and stir until the mixture resembles wet sand.

Once the water in the saucepan comes to a boil, add the remaining sugar and stir to dissolve. Add the rosewater, ground cardamom, and saffron paste, stirring to combine, then pour the mixture into the flour and butter mixture in the pot. Cook, stirring, for 2 minutes, until the mixture is syrupy.

Place the walnuts and half the pistachios in the bowl of a food processor and process until crushed. Add the nuts to the halva in the pot and stir with a wooden spoon for 1 minute until thickened.

Transfer the halva to an 8 x 12 inch (20 x 30 cm) baking dish and smooth the surface with the back of a spoon. To decorate, chop the remaining pistachios and scatter them over the halva in alternating lines with the rose petals. Cut into slices and serve.

The halva will keep in an airtight container in the fridge for up to 1 week.

Sholezard

RICE PUDDING WITH ROASTED RHUBARB

I worked on this rice pudding recipe with the delightful and talented Julia "Ostro" Busuttil Nishimura. In Iran, we have rice pudding for breakfast but the traditional version is a bit less exciting, made with water rather than cream and milk. We used saffron and rosewater but the vanilla is a new addition. Julia had the clever suggestion of serving it with roasted rhubarb, which brings a lovely sourness. These days I would never make sholezard without it.

PREP TIME: 10 MINS **COOK TIME:** 40 MINS **SERVES:** 6

1 cup (200 g) jasmine rice, rinsed
4 cups (1 liter) whole milk
Generous 1 cup (220 g) granulated sugar,
    plus extra for sprinkling
Pinch (1 g) saffron threads
2 vanilla bean pods, split and seeds scraped
2 teaspoons ground cardamom
2 rhubarb stalks, trimmed and cut into
    1¼ inch (3 cm) chunks
2 cups (500 ml) light cream
4 teaspoons rosewater, plus extra for drizzling
½ cup (65 g) slivered almonds
Ground cinnamon, for sprinkling
½ cup (65 g) shelled pistachios
Edible dried rose petals, to serve

Preheat the oven to 480°F (250°C).

Place the rice and 2 cups (500 ml) water in a nonstick pot over medium heat. Bring to a gentle simmer and cook for 30 minutes, adding the milk 2 cups (500 ml) at a time and stirring it through as the rice cooks. Add the sugar, saffron, vanilla seeds, and ground cardamom and cook, stirring frequently, until the sugar has dissolved and the rice is soft and broken down.

Meanwhile, place the rhubarb in a roasting pan and drizzle a little rosewater over each piece of rhubarb followed by a light sprinkling of sugar. Transfer to the oven and roast for 15 minutes or until the rhubarb is soft and cooked through.

When the rice is ready, remove the pot from the heat and stir in the cream, rosewater, and almonds.

Divide the rice pudding among serving bowls and spoon the roasted rhubarb, along with any cooking juices, over the top. Sprinkle the cinnamon, pistachios, and rose petals over the rice puddings and serve warm or chilled.

Shir Berenj

RAMADAN RICE PUDDING

This dish of shir (milk) and berenj (rice) is a very simple, traditional dish that's commonly eaten at the end of the day during Ramadan. People fast the whole day and, after sunset, when they can eat again, they like to start with something plain and sweet before moving onto hearty meat dishes.

PREP TIME: 10 MINS **COOK TIME:** 50 MINS **SERVES:** 6

1 cup (200 g) jasmine rice, rinsed
4 cups (1 liter) whole milk
Generous 1 cup (220 g) granulated sugar
1 teaspoon salt
⅓ cup (80 ml) rosewater
Ground cinnamon, for sprinkling

Place the rice and 2 cups (500 ml) water in a pot over medium heat. Bring to a simmer and cook for 30 minutes, until the rice has a pasty texture. Add the milk, sugar, and salt and continue to cook, stirring often to avoid the rice sticking to the base of the pot, for 20 minutes.

Stir in the rosewater, then divide among bowls and sprinkle cinnamon over the top.

"Persian cuisine is often humble in essence but with a love of lavish flourishes, and always served with pride, however simple it may be."

Party Time

*See over page
for dishes*

Party Time

When I cater parties, events, and picnics, these are the dishes I make. They are perfect for gatherings because they can easily be passed around on trays and eaten standing up.

HUMMUS

50

ZEYTOON PARVARDEH

olive and walnut chunky dip

48

DADAMI DIP

42

FELAFEL

56

NOON LAVASH

Persian flatbread

57

KOTLETS

Persian burgers

67

SAMBOOSEH

potato samosas

72

SOSIS BANDARI

Persian hotdogs

75

OLOVIEH

chopped potato salad

96

Drinks—especially tea—are extremely important in Iran. We drink tea when we get up, we drink tea before we go to sleep, and somehow no one ever talks of tea keeping them awake.

Every family has a kettle of gently boiling water going non-stop on the stovetop in their home. In the old days, we would have a samovar (traditional kettle) sitting over charcoal and on top of that there would be a teapot with black tea. These days, the smallest flame on our stovetop always has a boiling kettle and on top of that there is always tea brewing. My parents would easily drink 20 cups of tea each day.

As well as black tea (we rarely drink tea with milk), we have damnush (herbal tea), and I've shared some of my favorites in this chapter as well as a couple of cold drinks that fall more into the smoothie camp.

Alcohol is forbidden under Islamic law in Iran, which isn't to say that it's not sold and consumed in secret.

Drinks

Chai e Zafaran

SAFFRON TEA

I can't say enough good things about saffron, and Iranian saffron in particular—we think we have the best saffron in the world! We use it in savory dishes, sweet dishes, and even in drinks. It makes everything special, with its beautiful color and exotic fragrance. It is expensive but luckily you don't need much to transform a dish.

Black tea is ubiquitous in Iran but to make this common drink more special we sometimes add saffron to it. I serve this simple, healthy tea at my restaurant and everyone loves it. In summer, I often serve it cold.

PREP TIME: 5 MINS SERVES: 2

4 teaspoons black tea leaves
Pinch (1 g) saffron threads
1 teaspoon sugar (optional; see Tip)
4 cardamom pods
2½ tablespoons honey (optional)

Boil a kettle of water. Place the tea leaves in a teapot.

Place the saffron and sugar (if using) in a mortar and pound with the pestle to a form a powder, then transfer to the teapot. Pound the cardamom pods to a powder (don't worry if they're not completely ground), then also add to the teapot.

Pour enough boiling water for two people into the pot and stir in the honey, if you like your tea sweet (like I do). Leave the tea to steep for 5 minutes, then serve.

TIPS
The sugar helps to break down the saffron, but it's not essential.

If you'd like to make iced saffron tea, chill the tea in the fridge and serve with a squeeze of fresh lemon juice. At the cafe I've started serving iced saffron tea with soaked basil seeds, which adds another healthy dimension to this delicious drink.

Chai Beh

QUINCE TEA

Quince are such a lovely fruit but they need a lot of coaxing to share their most enjoyable qualities. Most of the time, we think about turning quince into jam (page 185) or slow-braising them in tas kabab (page 146), but I never let quince season go by without drying some as well. A quince infusion is so perfumed and wonderful, it's almost romantic.

PREP TIME: 5 MINS + 2–3 HOURS DRYING TIME **SERVES:** 2

1 quince

Wait for a sunny day, then, using a cheese grater, grate the quince and spread it out in a single layer on a large tray. Place the tray in the sun and leave the quince to dry out for 2–3 hours. Alternatively, you can use a dehydrator following the manufacturer's instructions or place the grated quince in a preheated 200°F (100°C) oven for 15–20 minutes until dry.

To make quince tea, place 4 teaspoons per person of dried quince into a teapot or cup and top with boiling water. Allow to steep for 5 minutes, then serve.

Chai Albaloo

SOUR CHERRY TEA

Whenever I think about this special fruit tea, I am always reminded of annual sour cherry-picking excursions with my brother. We had to pick bags and bags of fruit, enough for Mom to make the year's jam. We would always stop halfway through the day, make a fire, eat some cherries, and brew some up into a tea. When we got home, Mom would freeze some of our haul so we could have cherry tea year-round.

We traditionally drink this tea with sugar cubes: sweet and sour are always a good balance.

PREP TIME: 15 MINS **SERVES:** 2

1 cup (150 g) sour cherries
2 cups (500 ml) boiling water

Place the sour cherries in a teapot and cover with the boiling water. Allow the tea to steep for 15 minutes, then serve.

Ab Havij Bastani

PERSIAN ICE CREAM WITH CARROT JUICE

If I told you to mix ice cream and carrot juice you might think I'm a little strange, but you have to trust me here—this is one of the best combinations ever. Bastani sonnati (page 198) is Persian ice cream and if you head to that page, you can read about my long, hot, Tehran summers attending summer camp and the ice cream I always looked forward to having when my dad picked me up each day to take me home. If I really think about it, it wasn't just the ice cream that I loved, it was also this thick shake with carrot juice: it's one of the best taste and texture sensations in the world.

Dad would buy havij bastani from an abmive forushi (fruit juice shop), which specializes in juices, smoothies, and ice creams. This particular shop was called Abmive Forushi Moazeni, in Meydoon Hor (Hor Square), and the owner—we called him Amoo Seyfi (Uncle Seyfi)—had been there for more than 50 years selling havij bastani. There was always a line outside the front of the shop and it was always worth the wait—I can still taste it now more than 20 years later.

PREP TIME: 5 MINS **SERVES: 2**

2 lb 4 oz (1 kg) carrots, juiced (to yield
    2 cups/500 ml)
4 scoops Bastani Sonnati (page 198)

Divide the carrot juice and ice cream between two large glasses. Leave the ice cream for 1–2 minutes, until a little soft and starting to melt, then enjoy!

Majoon

BANANA, DATE, AND NUT SHAKE

When I look at this traditional Persian smoothie recipe, I actually think we invented energy drinks. Our aunties and uncles always told us this drink had health benefits, from regulating our body temperature to giving us lots of energy. In fact, they would tell us to never drink it in the evening because it would be impossible to sleep afterwards. In Iran, you will find this drink at any abmive forushi (fruit juice shop) but it's easy to make at home, too.

PREP TIME: 5 MINS **SERVES: 4**

4 cups (1 liter) milk (any type)
1 cup (100 g) walnuts
1 cup (140 g) shelled pistachios
2 bananas
1 cup (150 g) pitted Persian or Medjool dates
2 cups (270 g) ice cubes
½ teaspoon vanilla extract
½ teaspoon ground cinnamon, plus extra to serve
4 teaspoons tahini
Pinch of sea salt
Toasted sesame seeds, to serve

Place all of the ingredients except the sesame seeds in a blender and blend for 1–2 minutes, until smooth.

Divide the smoothie among four large glasses, top with a little cinnamon and a few toasted sesame seeds, and serve.

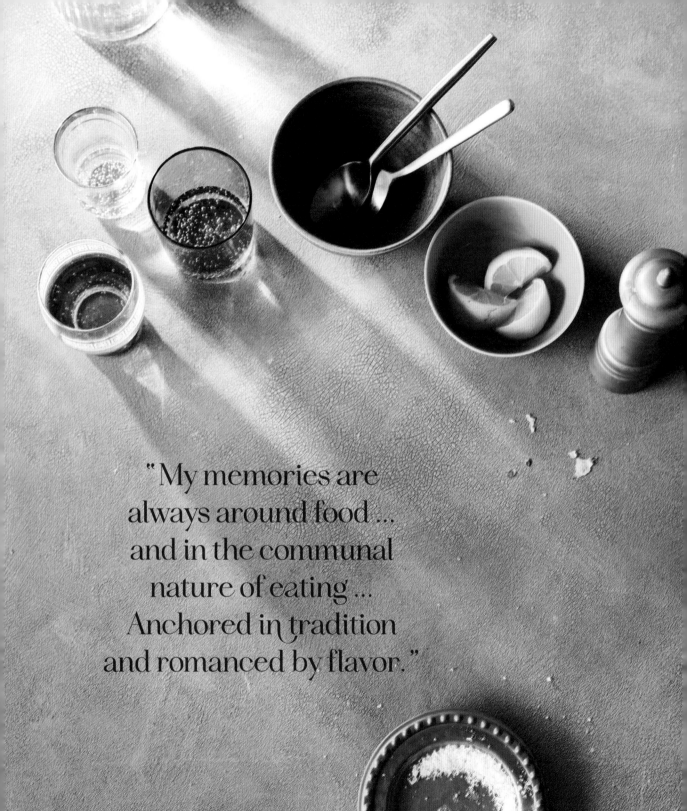

"My memories are
always around food ...
and in the communal
nature of eating ...
Anchored in tradition
and romanced by flavor."

Essentials

Saffron Liquid

MAKES ¼ CUP (60 ML)

Pinch (1 g) saffron threads
4 teaspoons granulated sugar
¼ cup (60 ml) boiling water

Grind the saffron and sugar using a mortar and pestle, then transfer to a heatproof bowl and stir through the boiling water to bleed the color. Set aside for 5 minutes, then use wherever a recipe calls for saffron liquid.

Saffron Rice

SERVES: 4–6

Rice is a key element of Persian cuisine and there are many polow (pilaf) recipes in this book. Alternatively, keep it simple with this saffron rice.

2 cups (400 g) long-grain basmati rice
1 x quantity Saffron Liquid (see left)

Cook the rice in a rice cooker or saucepan using your preferred method, then simply stir through the saffron liquid at the end for beautiful, easy everyday saffron rice.

Sabzi Khordan

HERB PLATTER

The classic Persian preparation of mixed greens—mostly herbs, scallions, and radishes—is sabzi khordan. My father would buy the ingredients fresh every second day and my mom would wash them and store them wrapped in paper towels inside plastic bags in the fridge. They'd then be pulled out to create this ubiquitous side dish or for a grazing platter.

We also wrap herbs and radishes in flatbread with feta—I think it's one of the best snacks you can ever have.

1 bunch radishes
1 bunch mint, leaves picked
1 bunch basil, leaves picked
1 bunch dill
1 bunch garlic chives
1 bunch flat-leaf parsley, leaves and stalks
1 bunch cilantro, leaves and stalks
1 bunch watercress (optional)
1 bunch scallions (optional)

Score a cross into the top half of each radish.

Clean any dirt from the herbs, then soak all of the ingredients in a large bowl of cold water for 15 minutes. Drain, then rinse and set aside to completely dry.

Roughly chop the herbs and scallions (if using) into 1½ inch (4 cm) lengths, then store the herbs, scallions, and radishes, loosely wrapped in a paper towel in a plastic bag in the fridge, for 2–3 days.

Enjoy sabzi khordan with your meal or wrap with feta in Persian flatbread for a tasty lunch.

طی شد راه دشوار آخر بر من و یار
چون بوسهٔ گرمی به او دادم
با لبهایی چون قند بر رویم زد لبخند
برد آن همه رنج و غم از یادم

Tey shod rahe doshvar akhar bar man o yar
Chon booseye garmi be oo dadam
Ba labhaee chon ghand bar ruyam zad labkhand
Bord aan hameh ranj o gham ze yadam

The last solution was over for me and my friend
Because I gave her a warm kiss
She smiled at me with lips like sugar
I forgot all the suffering and sorrow

فریدون فرخزاد
Fereydoun Farrokhzad

Thank You

Firstly, I would like to thank my mom, Farideh. Secondly, thank you to everyone who has been part of creating this book. To Jane Morrow and the team at Murdoch Books, thank you for bringing my dream to life. Thanks to Justin and Kristy for the editorial and design support, along with Lucy and Kirby for bringing the vision to life. To the photography dream team, Armelle Habib, Lee Blaylock, and the many skilled helpers, thank you for seeing the images in my mind and making them real. To Dani Valent, thank you for helping me turn my stories into words that speak from my heart. Last but not least, I want to thank myself, for believing in me, for doing this hard work, and never giving up.

– HAMED

Thanks to Hamed for trusting me with his important, resonant story, and for teaching me so much about Persian food. Thank you to Jane and the Murdoch Books team, for devoting heart, art, and resources to Hamed's beautiful food and stories. I also acknowledge my parents, Julie and Paul, who have their own stories of fleeing danger and persecution, and who brought me up to honor and welcome refugees. May our country do the same.

– DANI

Index

Published in 2023 by

Interlink Books
An imprint of Interlink Publishing Group, Inc.
46 Crosby Street
Northampton, Massachusetts 01060
www.interlinkbooks.com

Published simultaneously in the UK and Australia by
Murdoch Books, an imprint of Allen & Unwin

Publisher: Jane Morrow
American Edition Publisher: Michel Moushabeck
Editorial Manager: Justin Wolfers
American Edition Editor: Leyla Moushabeck
Design Manager: Kristy Allen
Designer: Kirby Armstrong
Editor: Lucy Heaver, Tusk Studio
Photographer: Armelle Habib
Stylist: Lee Blaylock
Food Assistants: Gemma Smith, Caroline Jones,
    Shannen Johnstone, and Josh Nicholson
Shoot Assistant: Zofia Harford
Production Director: Lou Playfair

OVEN GUIDE: You may find cooking times vary depending on the oven you are using. For convection ovens, consult the manufacturer's instructions or, as a general rule, reduce the oven temperature by about 25°.

Library of Congress Cataloging-in-Publication Data available
ISBN 978-1-62371-802-2

Color reproduction by Splitting Image Color Studio Pty Ltd,
Clayton, Victoria
Printed by C&C Offset Printing Co. Ltd., China

To find out more about our authors and books visit
www.interlinkbooks.com and sign up for our newsletters.

10 9 8 7 6 5 4 3 2 1